ENCOUNTERING THE WORLD WITH I-DOCS

Creative Research Methods in Practice

Series Editor: **Helen Kara**, We Research It Ltd.

This dynamic series presents short practical books by and for researchers around the world on how to use creative and innovative research methods from apps to zines. Edited by the leading independent researcher Helen Kara, it is the first series to provide guidance on using creative research methods across all disciplines.

Also available in the series:

- *Doing Phenomenography* by Amanda Taylor-Beswick and Eva Hornung
- *Fiction and Research* by Becky Tipper and Leah Gilman
- *Photovoice Reimagined* by Nicole Brown

Find out more at:

policy.bristoluniversitypress.co.uk/creative-research-methods-in-practice

ENCOUNTERING THE WORLD WITH I-DOCS

Interactive Documentary as a
Research Method

Ella Harris

First published in Great Britain in 2025 by

Policy Press, an imprint of
Bristol University Press
University of Bristol
1–9 Old Park Hill
Bristol
BS2 8BB
UK
t: +44 (0)117 374 6645
e: bup-info@bristol.ac.uk

Details of international sales and distribution partners are available at
policy.bristoluniversitypress.co.uk

© Bristol University Press 2025

British Library Cataloguing in Publication Data
A catalogue record for this book is available from the British Library

ISBN 978-1-4473-7416-9 hardcover
ISBN 978-1-4473-7417-6 paperback
ISBN 978-1-4473-7418-3 ePub
ISBN 978-1-4473-7419-0 ePdf

The right of Ella Harris to be identified as author of this work has been asserted by her in accordance with the Copyright, Designs and Patents Act 1988.

All rights reserved: no part of this publication may be reproduced, stored in a retrieval system, or transmitted in any form or by any means, electronic, mechanical, photocopying, recording, or otherwise without the prior permission of Bristol University Press.

Every reasonable effort has been made to obtain permission to reproduce copyrighted material. If, however, anyone knows of an oversight, please contact the publisher.

The statements and opinions contained within this publication are solely those of the author and not of the University of Bristol or Bristol University Press. The University of Bristol and Bristol University Press disclaim responsibility for any injury to persons or property resulting from any material published in this publication.

Bristol University Press and Policy Press work to counter
discrimination on grounds of gender, race, disability, age and sexuality.

Cover design: Qube Design
Front cover image: iStock/Veronika Oliinyk

Contents

About the author — vi
Acknowledgements — vii

1 Introducing i-docs as method — 1

2 Temporal architecture — 21

3 Spatial infrastructure — 37

4 Aesthetics — 51

5 Interactivity — 69

6 Co-creation and multi-perspectivity — 85

7 Thinking with i-docs — 107

Appendix: Interactive documentaries referenced — 121
References — 123
Index — 133

About the author

Ella Harris is an independent researcher with expertise in creative methods and 'crisis cultures'. She specialises in designing innovative methods that can help us make sense of changing socio-economic and cultural contexts by activating new ways of seeing, enabling meaningful co-creation, and producing impactful, interactive outputs. Ella is also the author of *Rebranding Precarity* and a co-editor of *The Growing Trend of Living Small*.

Acknowledgements

A book is always a product of thinking, imagining, and doing that extends far beyond its author.

Firstly, thank you to the participants who created the i-doc *The Lockdown Game* for taking a chance on the project and generously sharing their time, energy, creativity, and experiences to make it a resounding success. Thanks also to everyone I worked with when conducting the research that informed *The Temporary City*, and to the Arts and Humanities Research Council (AHRC) and the Leverhulme Trust for providing the funds that have allowed me to experiment with and develop i-doc making as a method. Funding aside, these experiments wouldn't have been possible without Michael Skelly, whose technical expertise, creative thinking, and appetite for challenge have underscored the success of both i-docs. A big thank you also to Jack Scott for fantastic artistic direction on *The Lockdown Game*.

I'm very grateful to Helen Kara for her enthusiasm and support for *Encountering the World with I-Docs* and her invitation to publish it as part of this excellent series. There are also many academic mentors to thank, including Beckie Coleman, who helped me to develop the concept and format for the book, Harriet Hawkins, whose work on creativity has been very influential in its arguments, Bambo Soyinka, who I appreciate for creating an experimental environment that's allowed me to test and progress ideas, and Judith Aston, who has been brilliant to think with in our collaborative work on i-docs. Huge thanks also to my boxing coach Chris Lodge, who's been a different kind of intellectual mentor. In guiding me from novice boxer to Elite National Champion 2023, Chris supported me to activate my potential in ways that have transformed my thinking (and also helped me to appreciate that while writing a book is hard, at least nobody is trying to punch you in the face while you do it …).

I'm hugely appreciative of all the friends and family who continue to support me through the twists and pivots of my ambitions. Special thanks to my parents Jenny and Oliver for instilling intellectual curiosity in me from day one, my siblings Mia, Nina, and Vivi for their love, friendship, and solidarity, Nigel for his quiet but steadfast support, and my 'little one', Jakhera Gilpin, for being a boundless source of inspiration, humour, fun, and kindness (as well as patience when I'm busy writing)!

And last, but very much not least, an enormous thank you to Kheron Gilpin, the best thinking partner I could ask for; always throwing me intellectual curveballs from weird and wonderful angles, always pushing me to excel, and always surprising me with the depth and detail of his love. (It's impossible to know.)

1

Introducing i-docs as method

> **Key chapter arguments**
>
> - Across history, human perception has been reformulated by creative media and technologies.
> - Creative methods can activate latent perceptual capacities and produce distinctive modes of attention for researchers.
> - Researchers can harness i-docs to develop and engage the ways of seeing needed to address contemporary questions and challenges, including intersecting crises and epistemic divides.

Our ways of encountering the world have long been shaped by creative media and technologies. From the printing press to the x-ray, to the camera, new mediums have altered not just our conceptual understandings of the world but the very nature of our perception. Montage techniques from film have impacted how we piece together memories in our minds. Novels have encouraged us to delineate life into chapter-like chunks. Social and digital media have led us to imagine ourselves as part of networks, much more than as part of spatial communities (Rainie & Wellman, 2012). And if you've ever had the experience (as I definitely have) of forgetting you can't *ctrl f* in a printed word document or call your house keys, then you know first hand how technologies reconfigure the ways we encounter the world. As media theorist Mark Deuze puts it, 'media structure our thoughts and actions', shaping how we 'grow up and learn, love, work, and play' (Deuze, 2023, 1).

This book is about a relatively new media technology, interactive documentaries (also called i-docs). It explores how i-docs can change our perception of the world around us. However, my aim is not just to describe the modes of encounter that i-docs enable, it's also to advocate for their intentional use as a research tool. I will argue that researchers can deploy i-docs to pay attention to the world in unique and generative ways. More specifically, I'll argue that the perceptual tools that i-docs offer as a research method are especially valuable in our contemporary era, defined as it is by multiple intersecting crises and growing epistemic divides. The book will provide a guide to making an i-doc, taking you through the steps required while also discussing how each of these steps might illuminate or enrich your research. I'll also show how just planning an i-doc, without making anything digital at all, can unlock many of the generative potentials of i-docs.

So what are i-docs? Well, that's debatable, and definitely debated by practitioners and scholars. For the purposes of this book, I'm talking about i-docs as web-based, non-fiction media that use both interactivity and immersion to engage users in a topic. If you've never engaged with an i-doc before, there will be lots of opportunities while reading this book as I'll be discussing a number of i-doc projects that you can visit online. You can find the web links for every i-doc I mention at the end of the book and I strongly encourage you to explore at least some of them while you read. Experiencing them first hand will hugely enrich your understanding of this topic. As you'll see, the examples I give take a broad spectrum of forms, ranging from sites that look a lot like a normal website, where you can pick and choose pieces of video, photo, audio, or text content to interact with, through to game-like platforms where you explore documentary issues by navigating content with an avatar and/or within the frame of a narrative.

Most i-docs are made by professional documentary makers and film studios and there is an international i-doc making scene. The National Film Board of Canada is a leading organisation in the field and has produced many of the most well-known i-doc projects. For example, their i-doc series 'Highrise' has been very successful. It comprises five i-docs, the earliest of which aren't currently available to engage with because they run on outdated web scripts (keeping i-docs alive online is a definite issue which I'll discuss later). The most recent in the series, *The Universe Within*, is a beautifully crafted, relatively high-budget project that allows the user to explore the digital lives of residents of high-rise buildings, guided by avatars 'made of code'. For examples of quite different i-doc projects, we could look at the much discussed *18 Days in Egypt*, a crowdsourced digital documentary about the Arab Spring in Egypt where users can upload their own footage and content. This much lower budget project prioritises social impact, offering a space for people's narratives of the revolution to be collected. I'll give many more examples throughout the book, but these give an idea of the range of projects that exist.

In my own work, I've developed the use of interactive documentaries as a research method. My first experiment with i-doc making, during my PhD, involved producing *The Temporary City* (password TTC),[1] an experimental exploration of the nature of space–time in London's pop-up culture.[2] My next attempt was a participatory i-doc, *The Lockdown Game* (press the remote to start),[3] made with a group of Londoners during the first and second COVID-19 lockdowns. Since then I've also used i-docs and i-doc-related digital tools within many kinds of research projects. For example, I've created interactive digital thinking tools to use in focus groups with arm's-length government bodies, I've produced gamified evaluation tools to use with children in pupil referral units, and I've developed interactive digital platforms for knowledge exchange and co-creative thinking as part of the AHRC-funded research and enterprise programme StoryArcs. In this book I'll talk about my experiences of i-doc making, while also discussing professional i-doc projects, to argue for their values as a research method. I focus on *The Temporary City* and *The Lockdown Game* as my other i-docs/i-doc like projects are

---

[1] www.thetemporarycity.com
[2] Please note there's currently an error with the map in this project.
[3] https://lockdown-idoc.netlify.app/

either incomplete and/or made for external partners with their own ethics and confidentiality requirements.

Many people would argue that the way I delineate i-docs in this book misses out on key areas of the field. For example, there is now a burgeoning subfield of interactive documentaries made with augmented reality (AR) and virtual reality (VR) technologies. Examples include *The Waiting Room*, *Witness 360: 7/7*, *The Chicago 00 Project*, and *Terminal 3*, as well as other installation and site-specific projects that could be categorised as interactive documentaries. There are fascinating projects within all these areas. However, I focus on web-based i-docs for two key reasons. One reason is that web-based i-docs are easier to make and to engage with than VR and AR projects (although that's changing rapidly as technologies become more cheaply available). They are also easier to explore for many users than location-based i-docs and installations, because they can be circulated quickly and easily online.

The main reason I focus on web-based i-docs, though, is a conceptual reason. I think that there are medium-specific ways in which web-based i-docs require and enable us to think and perceive that are valuable methodologically. That's not to say that AR, VR, installation, and site-specific i-docs don't have methodological values, just that their values as methods will be different to those I'm advocating for in this book.

There are also a number of interactive, digital factual media projects that don't refer to themselves as i-docs but are very similar in form and function. For example, *Going North* is an interactive oral history platform by Dr Charles Hardy III that presents stories from the first great migration to Philadelphia, US, using the capacities of an interactive digital platform to foreground the work of interpretation that shapes and mediates oral histories. Similarly, *I Can Almost See the Lights of Home* presents an oral history on a digital platform in a way that foregrounds exchanges between researcher and participant and offers a more dialogical way of encountering oral histories. The transmedia project RooTongue, a 'community gallery' that compiles accounts of endangered languages, could also be considered an interactive documentary, as could many more interactive digital platforms made by creatives and researchers.

In this book I'm not particularly concerned with drawing boundaries around what is and isn't an i-doc. My aim is to share the immense values I've found in working with a particular kind of i-doc as a research method in ways that I hope are accessible and motivating for researchers of all kinds. The one point of definition I do want to make is that, in addition to interactivity, i-docs need to be immersive in order to differ from a 'normal' website. Immersion is a form of attention that involves entering into a demarcated space (be that demarcation physical, virtual, mental, or atmospheric) and adopting an explorative, imaginative attitude within it. I've argued elsewhere that immersion involves an attitude of 'serious play' (Harris, 2017) where users/viewers/audiences are invited to take on an explorative and imaginative way of seeing. I-docs have many different ways of cultivating immersion but, however they do it, I think this immersive state is important in differentiating i-docs from other kinds of web platforms such as online news outlets or social media accounts.

Another thing I don't do in this book is rehash the body of work on i-docs from a media studies/digital cultures perspective. There's some fantastic work in this international field. In the UK, where I'm based, i-docs scholarship is notably supported by the i-docs research group based in the Digital Cultures Research Centre at the University of the West of England, Bristol. They were responsible for the first symposium dedicated to interactive documentary, convened by Judith Aston, Jon Dovey, and Sandra Gaudenzi in March 2011, and still serve as a focal point for collating and stimulating discussion around i-docs as a digital culture. Their website includes a bibliography section where you can find a long list of interesting and important work on i-docs. I'd really recommend exploring this work if you want to know more about i-docs. I've been involved with this research group, especially through my collaborations with Judith Aston (including organising a symposium on 'i-Docs Crisis and Multiperspectival Thinking' and writing related blogs and articles) and there are lots of interesting discussions and debates around the potentials of i-docs, as well as other documentary media, going on. However, there's no need for me to provide a full overview of a field that has already been summarised in existing books, articles, and edited collections (Aston, Gaudenzi, & Rose, 2017; Nash, 2022; Aston,

2022) my aim here is to focus on i-docs as *method* and in doing so to bring i-docs to researchers who aren't necessarily engaged with film and digital media as cultural forms.

I-docs as creative method

I-docs weren't developed as a research method. They evolved as an offshoot of traditional documentary film. Nonetheless, I'm not the first or only person to recognise their values within research settings. For example, the i-doc *One Shared House* explicitly functions as a research tool, gathering data about people's imaginations and desires for the future of housing. Within academic research, anthropologist Joe Smith led the interactive digital project Stories of Change, which showcases research to spark discussion about energy pasts, presents, and futures. The edited collection *Deep Stories* covers other anthropological experiments with digital storytelling and argues that digital stories can bridge 'separate domains of knowledge production' (Nuñez-Janes, Thornburg, & Booker, 2017, 7) as well as connecting 'people at a critical time of class, racial, and ethnic division' (15). I-doc making by academic, community, and creative researchers has been used for participant action research. For example, the interactive, co-creative online documentary *Quipu Project* was a vehicle for victims of forced sterilisation to tell their stories 'in a way that would offer them control in the process and would prove of value to them in their struggle for justice' (Cizek & Uricchio, 2022, 131). However, despite many clear overlaps between the agendas and mechanisms of i-docs and of research, i-docs have not yet been embraced as a methodology in the way that other mediums like film, photography, and even podcasting or comic books have.

I argue that i-docs can and should be part of the canonical repertoire of methods that researchers in all kinds of disciplines and organisations can turn to and experiment with. More specifically, I think they can happily belong within the growing body of 'creative methods' (Back & Puwar, 2012; Hawkins, 2015, 2020; Kara, 2015; Lury et al, 2018; Pink, 2001; Harris & Coleman, 2020; Benzon & Holton, 2021; Cizek & Uricchio, 2022). I-doc making is clearly creative as it involves organising and communicating information in imaginative and inventive ways. I-docs also belong with creative methods because they help us to attune to the world imaginatively. So far, when i-docs have been talked about as research methods, they've been put into proximity with visual ethnographic methods (Favero, 2013, 2017; Alexandra, 2017; Ryan & Staton, 2022) and considered as ways of undertaking participant action research (Mikelli, 2021, Cizek & Uricchio, 2022). In putting i-docs into the broader category of creative methods, I build on Harriet Hawkins' (2015) argument that creative methods can engage specific modes of attention to the world. In this article, Hawkins describes how drawing, as a creative practice, can focus our attention on aspects of the environment we might not normally be attentive to, such as light and dark and shape and shadow. My arguments about the capacities of i-docs follow this train of thought. As I'll show, aspects of i-doc making focus our attention on elements of the world that may otherwise not come into focus. For example, designing the interactive capacities of i-docs focuses our attention on tensions between freedom and compliance, while designing the temporal infrastructures of i-docs orientates us towards the temporal logics that define particular situations or phenomena. This activation of particular modes of attention is what I mean when I refer to 'encountering the world with i-docs'. The processes of i-doc planning and/or making, as well as the processes of engaging with an i-doc, change how we see the world by igniting, enlisting, and foregrounding particular dimensions of our perceptual capacities.

In her authoritative work on creative methods, Helen Kara has argued that 'Technology itself has an influence on people's creativity, yet the role of technology in the creative process has not yet been fully understood or theorised' (Kara, 2015, 6). In this book I undertake that theorisation for one particular technology – i-docs – showing in detail how i-doc making influences creative thinking. While Kara explains that creativity is hard to define, she identifies a common thread within creative methods as being the ability to defamiliarise topics and provide different, or multiple, perspectives on the 'truth' of an issue. The way that i-docs foster unique modes of encountering the world is certainly creative in this sense.

As creative methods have become more widely used within academic, community, and activist research, as well as within think tanks and charities, researchers have begun to experiment with amateur creative practices as well as to collaborate with professional artists and practitioners. These experiments have included drawing (Hawkins, 2015) working with audio (Butler, 2006; Gallagher, 2020), experimenting with comics (Peterle, 2021), photography (O'Callaghan, 2012; Simpson, 2012; Hunt, 2014) and film making (Pink, 2007; Lorimer, 2010; Garrett, 2011; Merchant, 2011; Jacobs, 2013; Garrett & Hawkins, 2014). An underlying premise to all these creative research methods is the conviction Hawkins articulates; that creative methods can help us to pay closer attention to aspects of the world that would otherwise be more elusive, including, for example, the sensory (Merchant, 2011; Pink, 2015) or the rhythmic (Simpson, 2012). Researchers argue that different forms of creative practice allow specific kinds of thinking to occur (Latham & McCormack, 2009; Hawkins, 2015). Video editing, for example, can be an analytic process through which 'sifting, sorting and composing' takes place (Garrett & Hawkins, 2014) while experiments with temporality in film and photography can tune in to non-linearity and processes of becoming (DeSilvey, 2007; Massey, 2008; O'Callaghan, 2012; Coleman & Ringrose, 2013). As Lury and Wakeford's 2012 collection *Inventive Methods* makes clear, 'devices' of all kinds, not just artistic mediums, can be mobilised to direct attention towards particular aspects of research subjects.

Other researchers have emphasised the power of creativity within activist and action methods, seeing their modes of encounter as valuable for *making* as well as describing and analysing the world around us (Kara, 2017; Pickerill et al, 2021; Pottinger, 2021). As explored by Cizek and Uricchio in *Collective Wisdom*, collaborative creative methods can produce a frame within which dialogue and change can happen. They can 'create inclusive and open design spaces where joint visioning and decision-making can occur' (Cizek & Uricchio, 2022, 91). In this book I'll argue that participatory i-doc making can harness this power for collective visioning. I'll show how the medium-specific capacities of i-docs can create a space for collective thinking and find common ground while also recognising and embracing difference and divergence.

Media technologies and the history of ways of seeing

While it's only relatively recently that the values of creative media as *methods* have been celebrated, there have been many more long-standing arguments made about the role of creative media as a cultural form in cultivating new modes of perception. These include explorations of how photography, cinema, the internet, and, recently, artificial intelligence (AI), are altering the ways we experience and understand the world. As Marshall McLuhan famously wrote, 'the medium is the message', that is to say, media technologies themselves, not just the 'content' they showcase, are meaningful and impactful. McLuhan writes that media are 'extensions' of 'our human senses' and 'configure the awareness and experience of each one of us' (McLuhan, 2001, 23).

There are obviously significant differences between creative media as used for research methods and creative media as produced and distributed within cultural and commercial settings. However, I think we can make many of the same arguments about both with regards to how they reformulate perception. Namely, both creative media and creative methods work to reconfigure the ways in which we understand, think about, and encounter the world around us. I therefore think it's important to locate i-docs not just in the context of creative methods but also to recognise their position in a history of creative cultural forms that have expressed and produced changes in the world and in our ways of perceiving it. As John Law has argued, methods do not stand outside of the social and cultural world, able to neutrally observe it, but, like creative media, are embedded in that world and inventive of it (2004). Crucially, the fact that particular media and methods have emerged at particular junctions in history – and in particular socio-economic and socio-cultural settings – is not incidental. Creative technologies have emerged from, and responded to, changes in those socio-economic and socio-cultural worlds. Understanding the values of i-docs as a method, then, requires thinking about the issues and 'structures of feeling' (Williams, 2011, 80) that define the era in which they've been emerging. This historicisation helps to emphasise their power as a way of cultivating the modes of encounter we need to understand contemporary issues.

In this book I'll argue that i-docs are responsive to an era defined by multiple intersecting crises that can't be meaningfully addressed partly because, as a global society, our convictions have become so polarised. I suggest that i-docs produce ways of organising and presenting information that attempt to make sense of this context. They do so by illuminating the complex intersections of issues and by bringing multiple perspectives about them into dialogue.

To enable a more precise analysis of how i-docs respond to and make sense of the particular conditions of the contemporary world, I want to draw out three key ways in which, across history, different creative media have responded to their own historical contexts. Firstly, I want to show how creative media and methods *create* new 'perceptual equipment' (Jameson, 1991, 80), allowing us to attune to changes in the world. Secondly, I want to show how creative media can *express* new changes in the world through the development of new forms of creativity. Then, thirdly, I want to stress that creative media also *produce* changes in the world, by making new ways to intervene in events and issues.

Creating new perceptual equipment

Fredric Jameson, in his influential work on postmodernism, argued that new media emerge when changes in society necessitate new 'perceptual equipment'. He asserts that if there is a 'mutation' in the world without an 'equivalent mutation in the subject' then this leads to widespread disorientation (Jameson, 1991, 38). That is to say, people's modes of perceiving must change as the world changes. For Jameson, we need creative media to enable these 'mutations' in us; to develop these new forms of perception.

Much work by other critics and theorists resonates with Jameson's idea, providing examples of particular creative technologies and creative forms that have made sense of societal shifts. Jonathan Crary, for example, argues that panoramas as an art form (huge paintings depicting panoramic views of a landscape) emerged in the context of disorientating, urbanising, 19th-century European cities and rescued people's sense of coherence by enabling them to piece together information that was too complex to take in all at once (Crary, 2002, 21). More recently, Tina Campt has explored how various contemporary Black artists, working within an era of continued struggles against racist and colonial structures, have created a 'new way of seeing' that challenges 'the dynamics of spectatorship and visual mastery' (Campt, 2023, 28).

These examples emphasise the role of creative media in making us receptive to the world in new ways; specifically, in ways that allow us to understand new and evolving realities. Placing i-docs in this lineage, I'll show how they enable us to be receptive to the contemporary world, defined as it is by intersecting crises and growing epistemic divides.

Many different terms have been used to articulate these processes of perceptual reformulation through creative technologies. John Berger's phrase 'ways of seeing' calls attention to the cultural, historical, class, and gender-based specificity of the various ways in which people encounter art and, through art, other people and places. Denis Cosgrove also uses the term 'ways of seeing' (2008) when exploring how techniques of geographical representation, such as maps and landscape painting, created distinctive ways of understanding the world before the era of mass travel and mass media. Art historian Jonathan Crary instead deploys the phrase 'regimes of vision' to foreground the historically specific modes of perception that are assembled by technologies of spectatorship in particular eras (2002). Specifically in relation to photography, Walter Benjamin famously deployed the term 'optical unconscious' to highlight how latent capacities of human perception can be activated through the camera (Smith & Sliwinski, 2017). In relation to more modern creative technologies, geographer James Ash (2009) has examined how video games make players alert to minute intervals of time, refining modes of encounter in an era defined by rapidly paced content (eg the short temporal windows given for Instagram or TikTok content).

As far as I've seen, work on creative methods rarely connects itself to this body of cultural theory on the reformulation of vision through creative technologies. And yet, the underlying assumption that creative media can create new 'perceptual equipment' is evident in most work with creative and inventive methods. For example, researchers have deployed video to produce sensitivity to rhythm in urban places (Simpson, 2012). They have also used comic books as a point of reference for developing a 'new optical unconscious' (Dittmer, 2010, 223) that can be more in tune with 'plurivectorial narration, simultaneity ... uncertainty, tangentiality and contingency' (234) and provide a 'practice of research that has the power to assemble and disassemble new spatial meanings' (Peterle, 2021, 1). The creative participatory art technique 'Exquisite Corpse' has been used to surface hidden values and perceptions in relation to ocean sustainability, cultivating a 'more affective relation to the concept of hypoxia' (Jung, 2022, 4). In his i-doc-like 'sociological web opera' *Paris, Invisible City*, Bruno Latour, collaboratively with photographer Emilie Hermant and screen designer Patricia Reed, uses interactive digital creativity to enable viewers to understand cities as assemblages of various trajectories (Latour, 2011, 91). All these creative methods work on the premise that new modes of perceiving the world can be produced through creative media.

In an era where life is now lived 'in' media rather than 'with' it (Deuze, 2011, 137) it's more important than ever to be intentional about how we perceive the world through media. My big argument in this book is that i-docs, as a relatively new media form, can be harnessed by researchers to generate some of the 'perceptual equipment' (Jameson, 1991, 80) we need in the contemporary era. As we will explore, the interactive, multi-perspectival, and co-creative capacities of i-docs can help us to untangle the complex trajectories of multiple entangled crises, see avenues for connection and collaboration, and create shared visions that accommodate differences.

Expressing changes in the logics of the world

Of course, one of the main reasons why creative practitioners develop these new repertoires of 'perceptual equipment' is so that, once they've attuned to their shifting environment, they can then communicate those changes to others. In his influential work on 'structure of feeling', Raymond Williams argued that the arts (eg literature, film, etc) are the first arena in which the defining logics of an era can be articulated. Before shifts in the 'cultural logics' of an era are documented in history books and political discourse, they begin to crystallise in works of art. This is because the styles and techniques of new creative forms can often mimic, and thereby begin to elucidate, the cultural or spatio-temporal logics of socio-historical settings. For example, Dada artists used collage to express 'the kinaesthetic jolts, estrangements and disfigurements of an increasingly unhinged modernity' in the early 1900s (Clarke & Doel, 2007, 598).

In *The Condition of Postmodernity* David Harvey traces changing conditions and conceptions of space–time through an analysis of their expression in creative forms. For example, he argues that Cubist artist work, which innovatively integrated multiple simultaneous perspectives within one perceptual field, responded to senses of fragmentation and multiplicity brought about by industrialisation in the early 1900s (Harvey, 1990). Likewise, he suggests that postmodern films like *Blade Runner* (1982) articulate the spatio-temporal conditions of the globalised world; developing a style that evokes the acceleration of turnover times, processes of time–space compression, and the unequal spatial relations in globalised cities (Harvey, 1990).

Film critic Joseph Fahim has examined how evolutions in Arab cinema have expressed changing socio-political experiences in the region in recent decades. For example, he explored how a wave of cinema burgeoned in the aftermath of the 2011 Arab Spring as filmmakers sought to capture and express a fleeting sense of personal and political possibility (Fahim, 2023). Fahim (2021) has also explored how experiments with the genre of horror have enabled Palestinian filmmakers to express the traumas of forced displacement. In the UK context, Dan Hancox has described early London grime music as creating an 'alien futurism' sound landscape, including by using sound effects from the video games consoles on which some early grime was produced. Hancox argues that this alien aesthetic expresses the structure of feeling in deprived areas of East London, where new, futuristic, skyscrapers were rapidly popping up on the skyline, visible from the rundown tower blocks in which many grime artists grew up (Hancox, 2019).

Creative media, then, provide a space where changing conditions and experiences of the world can be expressed. And, likewise, creative *methods* have sought to find the appropriate forms with which to communicate new realities. For example, Caitlin DeSilvey has approached climate change through experiments with creatively writing 'anticipatory histories' (including a co-edited book: DeSilvey, 2012). Or, the Stories of Change project, led by the Open University, involves an interactive storytelling platform that explores public stories around energy and community in the past, present, and future. Both projects use non-linear storytelling to evoke how climate change destabilises the relationship between past and future, undermining the metanarratives of 'progress' that have typified the modern imagination and demanding consideration of 'future unmaking' (DeSilvey, 2012).

In the vein of the work discussed, I think an exciting aspect of i-docs as a method is their ability to express conditions of the contemporary world. In particular, to express the interconnectedness of issues and people. As we'll see across the book, i-docs can draw attention to relationships across scales (eg between the personal and the political or the local and the structural), across geography (eg between experiences of citizens in countries around the world or between opposite sides of political divisions), and across time (eg relationships between remembered pasts and imagined futures). Equally, i-docs can express the complexities of tensions between agency, freedom, and compliance. Because they are defined by the agentic capacities they give and deny users, i-docs can show users how they are complicit in and/or powerful in the face of global issues.

Producing changes in the world

The ability of creative media to *produce* new perceptual equipment and to *express* changing realities undergirds their third power; the capacity to make change. Experiments with creative media and creative methods don't just make sense of the world, they also '*make* social realities and social worlds' (Law & Urry, 2004, 390–1). Law and Urry call this the 'ontology politics' of methods, a means through which realities are 'identified, labelled and brought into being' (392). Coleman and Ringrose echo this, arguing that methods should not only be understood as about epistemology but also as about ontology, because 'what is known is also being made differently' (2013, 397).

Of course, artistic experiments often have direct and explicit political aims. For example, the Bolivian team that made *Prison X*, a VR piece, explain their desire to mobilise 'theatre, dance, film, VR, AR, AI, Robotics, and other emerging mediums of communication' as 'tool[s] for decolonization', combating the use of these same technologies by dominant and oppressive geopolitical powers. In *Collective Wisdom*, Katerina Cizek and William Uricchio cite this and many other examples of co-creative media projects that seek to enact social change. This includes programmes made within the year-long National Film Board of Canada Program 'Challenge for Change', which included a series of documentaries made about Fogo Island, which were shown to government officials, ultimately leading the Canadian government to keep supporting the island, rather than resettle inhabitants, despite its low and declining population (Cizek & Uricchio, 2022, 86–7). In *Third Digital Documentary* Anita Wen-Shin Chang argues for the potential of transmedia art activism in 'decolonizing media practices, consciousness, spaces to imagine, invent and construct new realities, futures and ways of being' (2020, 13).

Like i-docs, creative methods are often mobilised with deliberate political intent. This is especially true within participant action research. For example, creative methods can be used to address inequalities by engaging publics who might not take part in traditional academic research. But political aims are also clear in other methodological experiments that don't directly frame themselves as action orientated. For example, Doreen Massey's creative methodological experiments with film, in collaboration with the filmmaker Patrick Keiller, sought to use film to expose the contingency of geographical orderings such as national borders and land ownership, paving the way for more inclusive communities. Researchers can also use creative modes of dissemination, as well as data collection, to political effect. For example, the edited collection *Oral History and Digital Humanities* uses a companion website to allow for an ongoing discussion of its contents, meaning that the book is no longer, then, limited to what is printed in it at the time of publication, but it has the capacity to evolve through online conversations and additions (Boyd & Larson, 2014, 6). In this way, the interpretations of data that the book offers are open to continuous discussion and contestation, removing the power imbalance that often comes with the researcher–community dynamic.

This third power of creative methods, to produce changes in the world, is key to what I think i-docs offer. Rejecting a history of scholarship that sees research as detached and impartial, I argue for i-docs as a creative method not just for grasping and expressing the world but also for intervening in it. This is, indeed, one of the most celebrated potentials of i-docs within scholarship in the field. Since their recognition as a new and distinct media form, i-docs have been seen as a creative technology that encourages users to 'get their hands dirty' (Favero, 2013). As we'll see, many i-docs explicitly invite users to follow-up links, contribute to surveys or petitions, share their opinions, form real-world connections with other people, and so on. In this book I'll explore how i-docs can be action oriented and foster collaboration towards change.

However, when considering the power of creative media and methods to produce the world in new ways, we need to remember that creative media can preclude and prevent change as much as they can enable it. Because creative media can, as we've seen, reformulate our modes of encountering the world, it's possible for them to change our perception in ways that acclimatise us to, and/or normalise, adverse socio-political conditions. For example, Crary's account of the panorama (which I discussed earlier) also exposes the role it played, as a new creative form, in acclimatising people to the sensory overwhelm of urbanisation by providing 'an imaginary unity'; offering an artificial coherence in the face of the actual incoherence of cities in Europe at that time. He argues that the panorama reconstructed a sense of order and overview, allowing the spectator to 'overcome the partiality and fragmentation that constituted quotidian perceptual experience' (2002, 21). Crary's choice of the word 'overcome' is interesting in this context. It suggests that, by offering a compromised sense of totality, the panorama played an almost therapeutic role in the face of an alarming spatio-temporal upheaval. But what if that sense of alarm was important for fostering criticality? For recognising the problems that urbanisation brought? There is a danger, perhaps, that in normalising new experiences and realities, we might pay less attention to the implications of those changes. This line of thought relates to arguments that media can be an 'opiate of the masses', pacifying people in the face of conditions they should be contesting. For example, does the acclimatisation to rapid intervals of time that James Ash argues video games cultivate make us less likely to contest the sensory and information overload that modern digital life entails? Does the feeling of digital connectivity that social media platforms produce make us less likely feel the loss of spatially defined communities? In exploring i-docs in this book, I'll examine how we, as researchers, can use i-docs intentionally to critically appraise, illuminate, and create changes, rather than to normalise them.

Why i-docs? Why now?

The previous sections should have started to explain why I think i-docs are valuable as a method. When deployed effectively, I think they can create new perceptual equipment that allows us to express and intervene in the challenges of the contemporary world. In particular, the chapters in this book are going to show how different aspects of i-doc making are helpful for approaching two key contemporary challenges; firstly, the 'wicked problem' of multiple intersecting and compounding crises (eg climate crisis, labour precarity, housing crisis, cost-of-living crisis, etc) and, secondly, the seemingly insurmountable 'epistemic divides' (gaps in what we think we know about the world and, furthermore, in what we think even constitutes knowledge) between groups in society.

The first challenge is something I've been increasingly preoccupied with as my work on precarity and 'crisis cultures' has developed. In my research into labour precarity, urban precarity, housing crisis, the COVID-19 crisis, racial injustice, crises in education (and much more!), I've seen how none of these crises can be understood alone – they are all entangled. Other recent social sciences scholarship has also been increasingly concerned with the complexities of living within intersecting precarities and crises (Lewis et al, 2015; Mulholland, 2020; Bowman & Pickard, 2021; Jones et al, 2021; Lombard, 2023). I contribute a constructive intervention to this work by showing how i-docs, as a multi-perspectival and non-linear medium, can allow us to pay attention to the mechanisms through which intersecting precarities and crises operate, are reproduced, and are contested. As I'll show, i-doc making allows us to refine our analysis of the systems and flows that create and perpetuate crises, pinpointing and articulating the details of how they operate.

The second challenge, of epistemic divides, is one that also concerns me deeply and that I've been exploring in my work to develop collaborative conceptions of story.[4] In an era defined by multiple compounding crises, widening political divides, and a 'post-truth' culture, we need ways of gathering and telling stories about the world that enhance understanding of intersection and connection, marry polyvocality with critical investigation, and enable compassion and collaboration between diverse groups. I show how i-doc making enables these crucial modes of attention. I suggest that i-docs can help to counter 'epistemic injustice' (Fricker, 2007) and produce knowledge in polyvocal but critical ways.

There is a growing body of work that examines how marginalised groups are disregarded as 'knowers'; excluded from knowledge production and deprived of the concepts they need to make sense of their worlds. These epistemic injustices hold us back from making sense of and navigating the complexities of multiple compounding crises. Within work on epistemic injustice, there is a call for methodological approaches that can produce knowledge in more epistemically just ways (Marovah & Mkwananzi, 2020; Cin & Mkwananzi, 2021). This book intervenes to offer i-docs as a method that can enable more egalitarian means of producing and sharing knowledge. I show how i-docs can contribute to efforts to co-produce knowledge with communities as well as to prioritise activist methods that drive progressive change.

What's to come?

In the following chapters of the book I'll show how the process of designing the various components of an i-doc – which I break down into their temporal organisation, the spatial layout of their interface, their aesthetics, and their interactive elements – engages and develops modes of attention that can be effective for approaching these two challenges of intersecting crises and epistemic divides. I also argue that co-creative i-doc processes can be used to counter epistemic injustice in social research and to build shared visions that accommodate, rather than eradicate or

---

[4] Within the project StoryArcs at Bath Spa University.

silence, divergent experiences and perspectives. Each chapter of the book explores a different component of i-docs and considers the modes of attention that designing that element of an i-doc can harness. Chapter 2 looks at the design of temporality within i-doc making and how this can elucidate the temporal infrastructures that shape social and political realities. Chapter 3 explores the creation of spatial i-doc interfaces (the layout of their pages and how pieces of content relate to each other) and shows how this aspect of i-doc making can develop our analysis of power dynamics and the reproduction of power through spatial relations. Chapter 3 then looks at i-doc aesthetics and shows how making aesthetic choices can harness critical attention to mood, structure of feeling, and, importantly, to how affect and atmospheres at different scales relate to each other. I then turn to an exploration of interactive capacities in i-docs and argue that designing interactive features helps us think about tensions between freedom and compliance. Chapter 6 discusses co-creative i-doc making to argue that participatory i-docs can enable people to find common ground even while giving space to different experiences and opinions. The book will conclude with Chapter 7, on 'thinking with i-docs'. Here I'll show how the values of i-doc making explored in the previous chapters can be mobilised even if you don't have the resources and/or the desire to make a digital i-doc. I discuss lower tech alternatives and also provide a template for planning an i-doc that researchers can use to engage the conceptual tools i-docs offer.

Although the book connects particular i-doc components to particular topics (eg temporal infrastructures to temporal politics, aesthetic elements to mood and feeling, interactivity to freedom and compliance) this is, of course, a mostly artificial separation. We can learn about collective moods by paying attention to temporality too, and we can learn about freedom by paying attention to aesthetics. I've divided up pairings in this way for structural simplicity, aligning each component of i-docs with the conceptual questions I think they are most suited to answering. But if you decide to work with i-docs as a method, please don't feel constrained by these groupings; there's no limit to what we can learn via the various elements of i-doc making.

As we move through the chapters, I'll be introducing terms that I've developed that can help you to understand the modes of encounter that i-docs engage. Some of these terms I've made up and some I've borrowed from other thinkers but brought into a new context. I hope they'll be helpful in clarifying what thinking with i-docs involves and why it is valuable.

2

Temporal architecture

> **Key chapter arguments**
>
> - I-doc making can help us to analyse temporality and its politics with precision.
> - I-doc making can help us to critique our conceptual assumptions and convictions about time.

Temporality

I'm going to kick off our exploration of i-docs and their modes of encounter through a focus on temporality. This is an intuitive place to start given that there has been a long-standing academic and cultural interest in how temporality is articulated and reformulated through creative media – in particular film – and, recently, through interactive and non-linear media (Crary, 1990, 2002; Harvey, 1990; Clarke & Doel, 2007; Clarke, 2007; Ash, 2009, 2015; Coleman, 2010, 2020a, 2020b; Dittmer, 2010; Bonilla & Rosa, 2015). It's therefore easy to add i-docs to this tradition and see their particular renditions of temporality as continuations of this technological and intellectual history.

Not all i-docs include film footage, although most have at least some filmic content. Regardless, i-docs are very much a temporal media. The pieces of content included in an i-doc will have their

Table 2.1: Key terms

Key terms	
Temporal architecture *Borrowed from Sarah Sharma (2014)*	In an i-doc, the temporal architecture is the temporal structure of the i-doc's interface – it's made up of the speed at which things happen, the options users have to skip, the times when they have to wait, the order they must do things in, and so on. This term is taken from Sarah Sharma's work on the politics of time.
Virtual *Borrowed from Deleuze & Guattari (1987)*	The virtual (following Deleuze and Guattari) refers to unactivated but real capacities of systems. For example, the capacity of water to become ice is a virtual property of water. The capacity of children to become teenagers is a virtual capacity of humans.
Actual *Borrowed from Deleuze & Guattari (1987)*	The actual (also following Deleuze and Guattari) refers to the virtual once activated; the properties of a system that have been actualised in a particular present moment.

own temporalities. For example, a film clip you add might have a particular pacing or you might include audio in the background that gives the whole experience a slow, contemplative atmosphere. But the temporality of an i-doc also, and perhaps primarily, comes from the design of its digital interface.

When designing an i-doc, decisions about the digital interface are grounded in decisions about how discrete pieces of media content are going to be laid out and related to each other. This layout is, of course, spatial – as we'll examine in Chapter 3, but it's also temporal.

Making an i-doc requires you to ask temporally oriented questions, as laid out in Box 2.1.

Box 2.1: Ideation notes for temporal architectures

- Should there be an order in which the audience is made and/or encouraged to look at pieces of content, or should it be up to them?
- Should there be pieces of content that can *only* be accessed after other content?
- Should all pieces of content be visible to the audience at once, or should they be on different pages or in different sections so that audiences are encouraged to watch groups of clips together?
- Should there be pieces of content that can only be accessed once, or for a limited amount of time, or should the audience always be able to come back to them?
- Should there be an introductory page or sequence to the i-doc and, if so, how long should the audience be required or encouraged to spend on it?
- Should the user have a limited amount of time in the i-doc? Does it 'finish' at a particular point or can they explore it indefinitely? If it does finish, how?
- Should there be any limitations on the amount of the i-doc's content that the user can view in one sitting? Are there things you don't want to give them time to watch or do completely?
- Should there be any restrictions on when the i-doc can be accessed?

These kinds of questions are how you start to design what I call the 'temporal architecture' of an i-doc. They enable you to decide on how to organise temporal aspects of the i-doc's digital platform (either by giving a design to a web developer or by creating it yourself). Answering these questions can also give precision to your analysis of temporality in research projects. Of course, there might be limitations to what you can achieve (depending on if you're working with someone who can code (or can code yourself), using an i-doc-making platform, or using some of the lower tech platforms I describe in Chapter 7), but i-doc-making limitations may prompt some generative questions in themselves!

Working out the answers to these practical questions will not only make your i-doc better for users, it will also help you to refine your analysis of your research topic. This is because designing an i-doc infrastructure that can communicate the atmospheres, cultural logics, personal/collective experiences, and so on, that define your topic requires you to pinpoint exactly what those are, and often to identify component features of them, so that you can express them via the i-doc. For example, if you were making an i-doc about experiences of medical care, you might ask yourself the questions listed in Box 2.1 and decide that you want to force the audience to engage with contents in a set order and limit their agency to the point of frustration to highlight experiences of waiting and dependency during medical treatment. These decisions about the i-doc would then reveal to you your convictions about this topic; that waiting and dependency are definitive aspects of that experience. Or, if you were making an i-doc about changes in the education system over time, you might debate whether to have a page for each decade, accessed in sequence so that users follow that history of educational policy changes, or whether to have a button that shuffles content, so that users get random clips from different years delivered to them. This internal debate in your head about the i-doc's design would also be a debate about what your key findings are within your research. The first option would be appropriate if you're making an argument about the progress of a particular policy or the development of a particular issue but the second might be more appropriate if you want to foreground commonalities between experiences of education over time or if you want to disrupt linear notions of progress in education. Your decision about the i-doc's temporal architecture would therefore refine your analysis of your topic's temporal dimensions.

I take the term 'temporal architectures' from Sarah Sharma's fantastic work on time. In her book *In the Meantime* (2014) Sharma develops this concept to make tangible the politics of producing and maintaining certain temporalities. Sharma describes how temporal architectures are composed of elements, including the built environment, commodities, services, technologies, and the labour of others; they are infrastructures that enable certain social rhythms to take place. In deploying this concept, she asks her own questions, including whose time is spent in order to maintain the mobility and recalibration of others, how are bodies 'differently valued temporally', and what temporal processes are employed to make people 'productive for capital?' (Sharma, 2014, 14). Using this concept and these questions, Sharma's book explores the 'expectation that certain bodies recalibrate to the time of others as a significant condition of the labor' (20).

From the early 2000s, research, including my own, has increasingly recognised the importance of temporalities, and temporal imaginaries, in how social life is organised and in how power relations are experienced and reproduced (Bauman, 2000; May & Thrift, 2001; Lefebvre, 2004; Bastian et al, 2020; Chan, 2020; Harris, 2020a, 2020b; Harris & Coleman, 2020). However, while there is recognition of temporality as hugely important, there is often a lack of precision in descriptions of the infrastructures and mechanisms of temporal systems. Sharma's work is an obvious exception to this, as the questions she asks in order to illuminate and analyse 'temporal architectures' help to give a detailed account of the temporal processes and orderings that produce and reproduce certain political realities. I think i-doc making enables us to do something similar, and to stay with these questions more easily, by engaging in a process of design that not only prompts these questions but necessitates that answers to them are clearly thought through – otherwise our i-doc won't work!

In the rest of this chapter I'll give fuller examples of how i-doc making can give precision to analysis of temporality. After exploring some interesting examples of temporal infrastructures in i-docs, I'll discuss the first i-doc I made: *The Temporary City*. I'll explore how making *The Temporary City* enabled me to analyse the temporality of pop-up culture as well as how to critique theoretical assumptions about time within my own thinking and that of my disciplinary home at the time (geography).

Examples of i-doc temporal architectures

One of my favourite i-docs is *A Journal of Insomnia*. Really I should say '*was*', because sadly *A Journal of Insomnia* can't be accessed online anymore. As I explained before, this is one of the current pitfalls of i-doc making; their lifespan can be dependent on the platforms and scripts used to build them. This i-doc is definitely still worth talking about though because of its unique temporality. Most i-docs can be accessed whenever you feel like it. But, *A Journal of Insomnia* is different. It has a landing page you can go to anytime, which introduces you to four characters. However, to learn about any of these people, you have to make an appointment to come back in the middle of the night. Once you've chosen your slot, for example midnight, you're sent an email with a link that becomes active at that time. This technique enables the i-doc to communicate the temporal experience of insomnia. The user has to wait to access the i-doc the way an insomniac waits for sleep; unable to drift off at will. Waiting until the middle of the night to watch it also immerses the user in the strange quietness of being awake while everyone else is sleeping. Furthermore, you can only visit one character at a time, highlighting the loneliness of insomniac temporalities; the detachment that comes from being out of sync with everyone else's rhythms.

Another interesting example of how temporality is approached via i-doc making is a common technique used in the projects *Hollow* and *The Last Generation*. These are similar i-docs about very different places. *Hollow* describes the story of population decline in McDowell County, West Virginia, US; an area that has seen booms and busts and, along with them, a population decline from a peak of 100,000 people to 25,000 at the time of the i-doc's making. *The Last Generation* is also about a declining place, the remote Marshall Islands, but here population decline is driven by climate change and the very real threat that this place might not be habitable within the lifetimes of the islanders' children. These projects are interesting to engage with together because they use similar design techniques to convey temporalities of decline. Both ask the user to scroll down and, as they scroll, information, clips, images, and so on appear, which tell the user more about these places.

The scrolling motion that users are asked to do complicates the temporality of decline. Scrolling down is associated with coming to the end of something, but as the user scrolls down these i-docs they learn more and more about the places, so their understanding accumulates rather than declines. In *Hollow*, scrolling down is literally scrolling towards the town's decline (captions appear on the screen showing years advancing towards the present day but population decreasing towards 0). Yet, because the user is learning more and more as they scroll, the town becomes more lively, vibrant, and complex for that user. In both these i-docs, scrolling is used to give nuance to how we understand temporality in declining places. It shows how, as these places near potential erasure, their stories take on heightened importance, making them in some ways fuller and richer.

Making *The Temporary City*: rationale

The Temporary City is the first i-doc I made. At this point, I was conducting my doctoral research into London's pop-up culture. Pop-up is a trend for temporary and mobile place making (initially including creative and commercial spaces like cinemas, theatres, shops, bars, art galleries and supper clubs, the term is now used even for welfare services including housing, courts of law and hospitals). If you're interested, I've written about it in my book *Rebranding Precarity* (2020). Pop-up culture took off after the 2008 recession as what I call a 'compensatory urbanism' (Harris, 2020b, 10, see also Harris, 2019) – a backup option for how to organise the city in the midst of crisis and recession. However, pop-up rapidly became a fashionable trend, and its roots in crisis were largely forgotten. Now, pop-up is a commonplace feature in cities around the world.

Time is important in pop-up culture because it is, ostensibly at least (my book complicates this), what defines its place making; pop-ups appear for temporary and sometimes unpredictable periods of time, repurposing empty shops or sites, or using buildings after hours. I was looking for a method that could help me to understand this temporal imaginary and what it was achieving in the particular socio-economic context from which pop-up emerged. I was experimenting with film making as a way to explore this.

While I was researching other peoples' uses of film to explore cities I came across some examples of early interactive documentaries and was struck by how their spatio-temporal format could mirror pop-up culture's own representation of the city as dynamic and unpredictable. I decided that I'd use i-docs as my methodology. I secured a place on an AHRC-funded training course in producing and editing film and set about making short films about a range of pop-ups in London. I focused on three types of pop-up place: shipping-container spaces, supper clubs, and cinemas. I visited these and conducted video ethnography as well as some interviews. I edited my clips using Adobe Premiere

Pro and also used Adobe Photoshop to produce collages for the i-doc (which I'll discuss later), using text, stills from my footage, and images from my online research. The clips I produced for the i-doc totalled 18 separate pieces of film, which, together, would take about 45 minutes to watch. I then worked with a technical specialist to create a digital interface to house and organise those clips. Luckily, the specialist I found was a friend of mine, Michael Skelly, who was happy to work on the project for the measly amount I was able to pay him with an additional AHRC grant (£750) because he was interested in the creative challenge. I planned the design of the i-doc and then met with Michael to adjust those plans based on what was feasible with the time and resources he could give to the project.

I won't talk at length about the methodological values of filming and editing as those processes have been discussed elsewhere by lots of other researchers (eg; Pink, 2007; Garrett, 2011; Laurier & Brown, 2011; O'Callaghan, 2012). What is worth focusing on here, however, is how editing clips to go into an i-doc differs from editing a conventional, linear film. In a linear film, you're assembling clips to produce a fixed sequence so are making decisions about what stays and goes as well as what order different clips should appear. However, when editing clips for an i-doc, you're not fixing an order. Instead, you're producing multiple discrete pieces of content that you know will have multiple different relationships to each other, depending on the pathways via which your audience accesses them. This changes the editing process; rather than putting the emphasis on sequence, the emphasis becomes on relationships. What should be foregrounded in each clip so that it relates, generatively, to other clips? What different meanings will this clip have depending on what the audience watches before and after? And how do you want to craft and curate those multiple potential meanings? For example, when I was editing one clip I produced about a supper club on a residential barge I realised that this clip would have different significances depending on if it was watched after another clip about a supper club or viewed after other pieces of i-doc content about the housing crisis. I edited the clip to retain both connections. In terms of temporality, this means that in editing an i-doc you're not telling one linear story, instead you're showing how particular scenes are simultaneously part of multiple, sometimes conflicting, trajectories.

Adrian Miles, an expert in online interactive video, has described the editing process as 'assembling particular sets of possible relations' (Miles, 2014, 75). I-doc editing then, is about contingency and multiplicity, it's about how multiple stories can unfold at once, and about how those stories can be experienced differently depending on what we interact with, in what order. This is one of the reasons why I think i-doc making helps to analyse temporal architectures; it helps us to get away from thinking about time as a singular linear sequence of events, and instead to think about systems as defined by intersections, multiplicity, and non-linear interactions.

I've used the terms 'virtual' and 'actual' – taken from Gilles Deleuze's philosophy (including his collaborations with Félix Guattari) – to understand this aspect of i-doc temporality. For Deleuze, the 'virtual' is different from the possible in that it already exists, even if it hasn't yet been actualised. Importantly, virtual capacities of systems that haven't been actualised remain real parts of the system and can be actualised later if the right interactions take place. For example, becoming ice is a virtual capacity of water. Even if water stays warm for centuries, it still has the capacity to become ice as a real property of that system. In i-docs, the different orders that content can be viewed in are virtual capacities of the i-doc system that are actualised when a user chooses that route. This is important because those different orders create different meanings. For example, say you're engaging with an i-doc about a protest and you watch a clip of one protestor talking about their experience before watching a clip of the march as a whole. You'll naturally see the march through the perspective of that person because of the order in which you selected content. But there will be other unactualised meanings that remain real – albeit virtual. For example, there might have been another clip about the policing of the protest, so if you watched this first you'd be looking at the clip of the march and noticing how it was controlled and maybe criminalised. These terms virtual and actual, as well as the term temporal architecture, will be useful in this chapter for understanding i-doc temporality and its modes of encounter.

Making *The Temporary City*: design

When I set about designing *The Temporary City*, I wanted the user experience (UX) to replicate the experience of pop-up culture. My design decisions were based around what would best represent its atmosphere. As I'll discuss, making these decisions helped me to identify particular 'logics' within pop-up culture (I won't talk about these at length here but in *Rebranding Precarity* I explore seven logics that i-doc making helped me to refine).

A clear example of how i-doc making helped me to elucidate pop-up's logics is how thinking about the i-doc's opening led me to consider immersion as a key logic. When thinking about how the i-doc should open, I decided to create a landing page with information about the i-doc that loads line by line (cultivating a cinematic feel) and then to offer an 'enter' button through which the user can travel into the i-doc itself. Initially, I labelled this button 'start', but I subsequently changed it to 'enter' because I realised that 'start' didn't give the feel I wanted. 'Enter' was much more appropriate in inviting the user into a demarcated space and into a mindset of serious play. This decision made me reflect on how important immersion is in pop-up cultures' spatio-temporal imaginary and led me to consider how this logic of immersion related to disorientation in the wake of the 2008 crash.

Once inside *The Temporary City* the user has two viewing options. One is a category view, giving easy access to any of the videos, but the user is encouraged to use the 'play' option, as this is much bigger and more prominent on the page. The 'play' page is a map on which icons appear indicating a type of pop-up (container, cinema, or supper club). Crucially, this isn't a static map; places come and go as time passes. The passage of time is marked by a calendar at the bottom of the screen. Its pages turn consistently, evoking urgency. I decided to set the rate at which icons appear and disappear quite fast so that not all the clips can be watched in one sitting as I felt that this was appropriate for pop-ups, which are always promoted on a 'come now or miss out' basis. There's no indication given to the user of which clips will disappear when. It's impossible to move backwards in time so if you miss one clip while watching another, it's gone forever

Temporal architecture

(unless you restart the i-doc). Again, I thought this was crucial to evoke the unpredictability by which pop-up defines itself.

Deciding how this combination of i-doc features would work together to evoke the temporality of pop-up culture was a key part of my research process. To work out what would best evoke pop-up culture's temporality I had to break down the component elements that give pop-up its distinctive temporal affects; how you can never seem to keep track of places coming and going, how they can be elusive and hard to access, and how they make and remake the urban fabric so that its continuously changing. This process enabled me to identify other i-doc logics: flexibility, secrecy, and surprise.

I-doc making also provoked questions I hadn't anticipated. For example, when I created my design, I completely forgot to think about if or how the i-doc would end, until Michael asked me what I wanted to happen once all the clips were gone from the map. Would the user keep exploring until there were no more clips available and be left in an empty map? Would the i-doc restart automatically? Or something else entirely? To answer this question I went away and thought about how pop-up culture itself would end, if it was to.

I realised I already had the answer to this. I'd been writing about how pop-up places ultimately displace themselves because they help to gentrify areas, which, in turn, encourages big housing developers to take over the land and produce expensive flats, kicking out the pop-up businesses that were there before. This is why pop-up became so popular with policy makers after the recession; it was seen as a route to encourage development in rundown areas. To reflect this I designed the i-doc so that after ten minutes exploring the play view the user is interrupted. A large text and image box appears with collaged images of flats under construction and a satirical notice telling visitors that their time in pop-up city is over because a luxury development is now being constructed. They're invited to visit 'pop-up city showrooms' and browse for apartments.

Designing this aspect of my i-doc's temporal architecture elucidated my analysis of pop-up culture as a 'compensatory urbanism' and helped me to understand the deep irony of pop-up's imaginary of urban space–time. While it presents a city that is always in flux, open to surprise, and inviting to small-scale intervention, its overwhelming function is to reinstate the primacy of large-scale private development. Pop-up is not a true alternative to neoliberal place making; it compensates for fractures in that system at times of crisis while ultimately working to fix those fractures. This helped me to understand that although pop-up's temporal architecture is defined by non-linearity and flux, it's part of a larger temporal system; a trajectory towards the totalising financialisation of urban space.

Problematising assumptions about temporality

I hope the examples I've given show how valuable i-doc making is in focusing attention on temporal architectures and their politics within particular research topics. In this section, I want to show how i-doc making can also help to critique our conceptual assumptions and convictions about time. I-docs have been conceptualised as more than 'the extension of linear documentary into digital media' and as 'something else' entirely (Gaudenzi, 2013, 12). A vital aspect of this 'something else' that i-docs offer is a politics that hangs on multiplicity, contingency, and the ability 'to change and evolve' (Gaudenzi, 2013, 13). Scholars argue that, as a film form typified by modularity, variability (Gaudenzi, 2013), complexity, and choice (Nash, 2022), i-docs allow multiple and open-ended narrativisations of the topics they explore. For example, they mobilise interactive elements, including user-generated content, to destabilise representations of socio-political and environmental issues such as the Arab Spring (*18 Days in Egypt*), urban shrinkage (*Hollow*), or energy futures (*Journey to the End of Coal*). If you summarised scholarship on i-docs you'd conclude that there is something distinctively progressive about their non-linear formats; that presenting an issue through an i-doc will be, almost inherently, a critical analysis of that issue.

These assumptions about the politics of i-docs as a non-linear medium echo assumptions within much contemporary theory. Geography, the discipline within which I did my PhD, has been especially influenced by Deleuze's characterisation of space–time as non-linear, creative, dynamic, and unpredictable. This conception of space–time can be found at the core of many contemporary theoretical approaches in geography and related disciplines including assemblage theory (Bennett, 2005; Anderson & McFarlane, 2011; McFarlane, 2011), vital materialism (Bennett, 2010), studies of turbulence and disorder (Cresswell & Martin, 2012), and the relational ontology key to Doreen Massey's important work (Massey, 2005).

Within a lot of this work there's an association made between non-linearity and progressive politics. Yet, non-linearity doesn't always equate to leftist or progressive agendas. As Eyal Weizman has discussed, the Israeli Defence Force (IDF) explicitly incorporate Deleuzian 'principle[s] of nonlinearity' in their training, encouraging soldiers to conceive of the city as 'a flexible, almost liquid medium that is forever contingent and in flux' as well as to advance an approach to battles that assumes no predetermined narrative but rather an unpredictable order of events (Weizman, 2006). The fact that these non-linear logics can be employed towards the military practices of the IDF makes pertinent the kind of analysis that I think i-docs enable; an attention to non-linear temporalities that doesn't presume a particular politics but carefully examines their development and implications in specific contexts. All i-docs are non-linear, but rather than assuming a political meaning goes along with this, we can use i-doc making to focus on the specific and localised ways that non-linear temporality manifests in a particular context.

Making *The Temporary City* definitely helped me to have a more astute understanding of the politics of pop-up culture's non-linear temporal imaginaries. When I started my PhD, I'd assumed that pop-up culture would be something interventionist, even revolutionary; offering everyday people a chance to remake their cities. I assumed this because I'd been working in Cairo during the Arab Spring and seen people using pop-up film screenings (although they didn't call them that) to highlight and contest human rights abuses. However, as I've already started to explain in relation to the i-doc's ending, making *The Temporary City* helped me to understand how pop-up compensates for and reinstates, rather than contests, the neoliberal city.

Other than the i-doc ending, the other feature that helped me to interrogate pop-up's politics was the 'outside pop-up city' pages. These are collages I made on Photoshop using images from the internet as well as stills from my own footage. While the video clips mostly present pop-up places as they want to imagine themselves – as trendy, exciting places to visit – the outside-pop-up city pages bring out contexts and themes that problematise pop-up's presentation of itself. It was through these collages that I mapped out how pop-up relates to the crises and precarities that ensued after the 2008 crash: labour precarity, the housing crisis, and opportunistic gentrification.

In the i-doc, the outside pop-up city pages appear as links at the end of certain clips. For example, one clip is about Artworks: a shipping-container shopping mall and entertainment space. In the clip we see people having a drink outside one container space. As the camera pans up, building works are visible in the background. At the end of the clip the user is offered an option to see 'outside the pop-up city'. If they choose this they get a pop-up box with a collaged image which includes text explaining that the Artworks occupies the site of the Heygate Estate, a council estate that was very controversially decanted and demolished to make way for expensive flats, with the residents displaced across the country. The new context offered by the outside pop-up city page might make the user reflect on the building works going on in the background of the container mall. Making these pages helped me to construct a picture of what's left out of pop-up's own self-depiction and why. In this instance, it illuminated how pop-up's flexibility logic – which imagines the city as a malleable surface where places can come and go unpredictably – actually deploys this non-linear imaginary to justify the displacement of social housing tenants. Because the outside pop-up city pages are offered as one of two or more optional links, the user might not discover them and learn about these political contexts of pop-up culture. Nevertheless, these realities remain a real part of the system – a virtual capacity that can be activated within another encounter. This reflects how problematic political implications of urban cultural phenomena persist even when they're not acknowledged within our narratives of the city.

Including the outside pop-up city pages was important in ensuring my i-doc critically attuned users to pop-up culture rather than normalised its logics. Earlier, I discussed Crary's argument that creative media can 'overcome' disorientating spatio-temporal sensations such as fragmentation by providing a perceptual apparatus that makes sense of them. I suggested that this raises concerns around how creative media and methods could acclimatise us to troubling conditions and thereby reduce our desire and ability to respond to them critically. This is something that I have been careful, in developing my own use of i-docs, to avoid. In *The Temporary City* the outside pop-up city pages make sure that the i-doc doesn't simply reproduce pop-up culture's atmospheres uncritically – acclimatising users to it – but instead prompts users to see outside of that imaginary and critique its implications. In doing so, the i-doc also helps to critique disciplinary assumptions that non-linear logics are always conducive to progressive politics, as is indeed often assumed of pop-up by those who take its imaginaries at face value.

So as we've seen, i-doc making can be a fantastic method for exploring temporal architectures with precision. We've also seen how i-doc making can enable us to interrogate our own disciplinary or ideological assumptions about temporalities and their values.

While filmmaking has long been used to explore temporality, duration, and becoming, i-doc making offers a different kind of temporal analysis. It allows us to identify the exact elements that make up temporal architectures and the exact mechanics of their functioning. This then enables us to examine and problematise the relationships between temporalities and political or socio-economic realities.

3

Spatial infrastructure

> **Key chapter arguments**
>
> - I-doc making can shed light on the relationship between power and space.
> - Designing the spatial infrastructure of an i-doc can illuminate politicised tensions between fluidity and fixity.

Spatial infrastructures

We started with time because of the close relationship between film technologies and theories of temporality. Designing the spatial layout of an i-doc is, however, foundational to the modes of thinking and encountering that i-doc making catalyses. By spatial infrastructure, I mean the way that an i-doc's pages are laid out on a screen, how content is arranged within those pages, and how content is linked together within and across pages. In this chapter we'll see how playing close attention to spatial infrastructure design can draw attention to how power dynamics are embedded spatially. By 'spatially' I'm not just referring to how power dynamics correspond to spatial markings – for example, borders, boundaries, locations, and routes in geographical space – although this is certainly a dimension. I'm also talking

Table 3.1: Key terms

Key terms	
Attractors *Borrowed from Manuel DeLanda (2013)*	This is a term that Manuel DeLanda has used in his explanations of Gilles Deleuze's philosophy. Attractors are points or elements in an environment that attract the trajectories of a system. They are useful for explaining why actions often follow a particular course even though systems are ontologically open. For example, a deeply dug channel might attract water to follow a particular course again and again, even though that course is hypothetically open to change.
Discovery pathways *My invention*	A route or mechanism through which the user is encouraged to navigate the i-doc interface and comes across i-doc content.

about mobility and fixity, stability and fluidity, and about people's agencies, imaginations, and desires in relation to place and space.

Space and power are key topics in social sciences research. Doreen Massey's crucial work on 'power-geometry' (Massey, 2005) has helped researchers pay attention to how power is embedded in distributions of space as well as in spatial flows and blockages (Belanger & Silvey, 2020; Bissell, 2021), while other work has mobilised assemblage theory to understand patternings of power through spatial configurations (Allen, 2011; Anderson & McFarlane, 2011; Harris et al, 2020). I argue that processes of i-doc design and creation can give more precision to our understanding of power geometries, the role of different agents within them, and pathways for their re-assemblage.

In this chapter I'll discuss three case studies to show how different spatial infrastructure designs elucidate power geometries. These will be: *Gaza Sderot*, an i-doc about lived experiences of the Israeli occupation of Gaza; *Refuge Republic*, which offers users different walks through Camp Domiz (a Syrian refugee camp in Iraq); and the second i-doc I made, *The Lockdown Game*, which my participants designed in a way that foregrounds the sharp distinction between indoor spaces of the home and the outdoor world during the COVID-19 lockdown in London.

Spatial infrastructure

Some i-doc theorists have aimed to create a typology of i-docs. Often such typologies differentiate i-docs by their spatial infrastructures. For example, Kate Nash (2022) explores the database as an important influence for one kind of i-doc. The database structure is an important reference point for i-docs as it's enabled the medium to move beyond narrative as a structuring device and instead open up space for a multiplicity of parallel experiences.

There are indeed a variety of 'types' of spatial interface in i-docs. For example, i-docs about a particular place often use a map as the basis of their interface design, while 'database' i-docs simply structure their interfaces as a page of clips from which users can select. Others invite users into a game-like world that can be explored, with pieces of content linked to pinpoints or objects within that world. Some i-docs have one main page of their interface, with more content revealed as you scroll down or across, or as you click through or watch content. Others have multiple pages that can be accessed from a landing page or by using tabs.

So, what kinds of questions and decisions are involved in designing an i-doc's spatial infrastructure. As with designing the temporal architectures of i-docs, the spatiality of an interface should have some relationship to the spatial logics of your topic. (I say should. Clearly it doesn't *have* to, but my conviction is that the best i-docs, and indeed the best examples of most art forms, have an intentional relationship between form and meaning. Certainly from a researcher's perspective, the questions about meaning that are prompted by decisions about form are what I think are most valuable in i-doc making.) Designing your interface requires reflecting on the spatial logics that define your topic.

The kinds of questions you might ask yourself as you design your i-doc interface include those outlined in Box 3.1.

Box 3.1: Ideation notes for spatial infrastructures

- Should all the content be visible at once on the same page, or do you want the user to have to discover content?
- If the latter, what should the pathways to discovery be? Is the user required to scroll down, up, or through content (either moving to

the right or to the left), or do they click between different pages to see groupings of content? Or are there a combination of different 'discovery pathways'?
- Should content be visible immediately or revealed by clicking on an icon or object? If the latter, what should these icons or objects be?
- Should the layout of the interface be stable, or do you want pieces of content to move around depending on what the user does?
- Do you want to use a map, diagram, chart, list, or some kind of other structuring device to show relationships between and/or groupings of pieces of content?
- What kind of screen-based media do you want your interface to mimic? A game? A database, article, timeline, video game, map?
- Do you want more than one option for how users encounter content? For example, a map view and a database view? Or a page that structures content along a timeline and then another page that groups it thematically?

Interfaces and power geometries

In this section we'll explore how answering questions of these kinds can help to think about spatial patternings of power, through an analysis of our three examples. I'll start with the two map-based i-docs I already mentioned, as these are excellent examples of how i-doc interfaces are used to express the spatial constitution of power. *Gaza Sderot* sadly can't be accessed fully anymore as it runs on a defunct version of JavaScript, but *Refugee Republic* is available for free online.

Gaza Sderot's full title is *Gaza Sderot: Life in Spite of Everything*.[1] It was an ambitious interactive documentary project, created by teams from both Palestine and Israel, in connection with B'Tselem (Israeli Information Center for Human Rights in the Occupied Territories).

---

[1] My analysis of *Gaza Sderot* was written before the 2023/24 war on Gaza and therefore doesn't address the i-doc in the context of the current genocidal attacks.

From 26 October to 23 December 2008, two videos were posted per day, resulting in 80 videos hosted in the i-doc by the end of the period. Two further clips were created and added by the teams following Israel's war on Gaza in 2008/09. The project's aim was to 'report on life as experienced by men, women and children in Gaza (Palestine) and Sderot (Israel): their lives and their survival on a daily basis'. It followed six people from Gaza and six from Sderot.' The daily video posts allowed viewers to follow these people 'intimately for 10 weeks' as well as to have 'personal, interactive and nonlinear access to contents on the site', including videos, blogs, a discussion forum, links, and so on. The i-doc can be watched in English, French, German, Arabic, or Hebrew.

Gaza Sderot's interface has four different screen options that users can choose from, in order to access its contents. These are a map view, a timeline view, a face view (that filters by person), and a topic view. In many ways, all four options emphasise the liveliness of space, reminding viewers of the lives lived 'in spite of everything'. For example, in the map view, clips are labelled with captions such as 'ambulance drivers' HQ' or 'new apartment of Daniel's sister' – descriptions that emphasise space as something constituted by peoples' activities and actions. Clicking on any of the displayed clips makes them start to play and instantly converts the static map into a dynamic, spatio-temporal fabric, as it portrays the activities of the characters.

Geographer Doreen Massey conceptualised space as 'a simultaneity of stories so far', because it is continually shaped by the interconnected practices of various actors (Massey, 2005, 9). In *Gaza Sderot*, the videos embedded in the map evoke a similar conception of space–time. Clip descriptions correspond to the ways that spaces are utilised by people (eg 'polling place' or 'Ahmed Quaffah's Party') while official place or road names have been omitted. This nomenclature conveys an imaginary of space as created through people's stories.

The face view, adopting a biographical approach to the i-doc's video material, reinforces this notion of space as lively. When you navigate the i-doc through 'faces' it unveils the complete cast of people the i-doc follows. When you watch the clips they don't open full screen but remain in place among the other faces. This highlights that the person whose life you're currently learning about is one of many simultaneous stories co-creating the geographies of Gaza and Sderot.

Yet, this coexistence of stories alongside one another also reiterates the inability of individuals to extract their own worlds from that of the occupation. It's impossible to zoom into one person's story and forget about the political context. You can only watch their clips in small windows visible within the wider screen view showing those they live amongst, either side of the border.

A concept I've found helpful to understand spatial infrastructures is that of 'attractors'. This is a term that Manuel DeLanda has used in his explanations of Gilles Deleuze's philosophy. Attractors are points or elements in an environment that attract the trajectories of a system. They are useful for explaining why actions often follow a particular course even though systems are ontologically open. For example, a deeply dug channel might attract water to follow a particular course again and again, even though that course is hypothetically open to change. In *Gaza Sderot*, the interface provides multiple attractors that pull the user away from following the story of any one person. Not only do other clips remain visible as you engage with any one person's story, but suggested links at the end of clips move your attention to things that happened before, after, elsewhere, or to someone else. These competing attractors emphasise the strain of life lived within the power geometries of the occupation.

What's more, the overbearing force of the occupation in ordering lives lived in this space is demonstrated in *Gaza Sderot*'s interface by a line down the middle of the screen that separates the clips in Gaza from those in Sderot. The line is present and unwavering in all four of the i-doc screen views and has no interactive capacities. There is nothing you can click on, hover over, or open up to get rid of the line. In this way it suggests the totalising force of this ordering of space. The line is an attractor so strong that all content, and all pathways through that content, are shaped by it.

In combination then, the features of *Gaza Sderot*'s interface communicate its understanding of space and power, portraying a geography that is at once lively – made up of the agency of multiple individuals – and fixed – stuck within the divisions of a devastating occupation with no end in sight.

Refugee Republic

Refugee Republic, like *Gaza Sderot*, uses a map-based interface but does it somewhat differently. Its main page offers a hand-drawn sketch map of the refugee camp, Camp Domiz. When you hover over the map different 'routes' illuminate: 'camp construction route', 'camp money route', 'camp smart route', and 'camp life route'. Clicking on one of these routes activates a 'walk' – taking you to a scroll-through sequence of video clips, audio, still images, sketches, and diagrams.

The stated aim of the i-doc makers was to 'enrich the existing image of refugee camps by building an anatomical sketch of everyday life in the camp, through a combination of drawings, film, photography, sound and text to create a sensory experience'. Indeed, each walk shows the vibrancy and complexity of camp life, where children go to school, couples get married, people open shops, start businesses, and so on.

By making 'routes' the primary pathway of discovery, this i-doc emphasises motion, reiterating that camps are dynamic places where full lives are lived. However, as in *Gaza Sderot*, there is a tension between fluidity and fixity emphasised by this interface design too. While there are four routes to choose from, there are no routes out of the camp; no onwards passage to any external destination. This sheds a different light on the i-doc's portrayal of the vibrancy of camp life, showing how people are forced to construct homes and organisations, make money, educate themselves, and live out their lives in these permanently temporary spaces because of the lack of a way out.

Other elements of the i-doc's interface and contents reiterate this point. At the bottom of the screen there is a rolling 'camp news' banner that shows the numbers registered in the camp and how much over capacity this is, reminding us that, while people are constantly arriving, leaving is much harder. The sketches and diagrams you visit on the 'walks' through the routes also explore tensions between movement and fixity. For example, one sketch in the 'camp construction route' includes an annotation that questions 'when does a structure become a house?' – exploring the nebulous line between temporary shelter and long-term home. Another sketch of a community space is annotated with the comment 'this is not a bus stop but a community space'. The comment doesn't just draw attention to the structural similarity to a bus stop but also to the irony of building a community space that looks like a bus stop in a community where everyone is hoping to leave.

In both these i-docs, map-based interfaces are used to show tension between fluidity and fixity and to relate these to distributions of power. In *Gaza Sderot*, the dominating, immutable force of the line expresses the totalising force of the Israeli occupation of Gaza on the lives of people on both sides. In *Refugee Republic*, the irony of structuring the interface around routes – when the i-doc is about a place people mean to pass through but end up building their lives in – foregrounds an irony in power and agency. It shows how refugees are robbed of agency as they become subservient to the decisions of governments and the benevolence of multinational charities and organisations, but are also simultaneously required to step into their agency in order to build meaningful lives with limited resources and construct a society with ad hoc infrastructures.

The Lockdown Game

I'm now going to turn to *The Lockdown Game*, a participatory i-doc that I made with a group of 13 Londoners during the COVID-19 pandemic, along with artistic lead Jack Scott and technical lead Michael Skelly (who also worked on *The Temporary City*).

The design process for this i-doc was very different to *The Temporary City*. Rather than me making decisions about how the i-doc could express pop-up culture by myself, my participants worked together to decide what kind of i-doc would best express their experiences of lockdown. As I'll show, their own encounter of lockdown through i-doc making helped them to analyse (among other things) the power geographies of the situation.

The Lockdown Game wasn't actually the i-doc I set out to make. I had funding (a Leverhulme Early Career Fellowship) to make an i-doc about class politics on local highstreets in London. I'd recruited a group of participants from Deptford and from Dalston (areas of London) who were ready to take part in this study. However, when lockdown was imposed in March 2020, my project, along with so many other plans, was made impossible. Thirteen of my participants agreed to take part in a revised project that would still involve i-doc making but would do so via online activities and would explore experiences of lockdown instead. They were a diverse group in terms of age, gender, ethnicity, class background, and occupation, but the participants were all living in either Deptford in South East London or Dalston in North East London. My initial idea was that the i-doc would be about how experiences of lockdown were differentiated by class but, as the project progressed, it became clear that imposing my own research agenda in this setting was impractical, if not unethical. The group, like everyone else in that period, needed time and space to process their experiences of lockdown in an explorative fashion, not to be curtailed by the research questions of an academic. I ended up leaving it to the group to decide what they recorded, how they designed the i-doc, and what they wanted to communicate through that process.

I planned out a year-long process for participatory i-doc making, divided across a series of stages. Firstly, I asked the group to record content about their experiences of lockdown with whatever medium they felt comfortable. The materials they produced included photography, video, collage, music, and writing. I then arranged three Zoom workshops. At the first I did a presentation for the group about what i-docs are, the various different ways they can be designed, and what I thought we might learn by making one together (the presentation was sort of a very minimal version of this book). The intention with this was to give my participants an idea of the scope of i-docs, spark ideas for their own design, and emphasise that the process of making the i-doc would also be a process of analytical discovery about their individual and shared experiences. At this workshop my participants also introduced themselves and presented the content they'd made to each other. Their content was also available for them to browse before and after the Zoom meeting in a mutually accessible Google Drive folder.

At the second Zoom workshop I split the participants into three breakout groups that were responsible for designing different elements of the i-doc. Participants had the option to state their preference of group or to be randomly allocated. One group was in charge of the 'infrastructure' design (which incorporated what I've defined in this book as temporal architectures and spatial infrastructure), one was in charge of aesthetics (including colour schemes, fonts, soundscapes, style, etc), and the third was in charge of the i-doc's interactive features (what should be clickable, what prompts, questions, or demands the user should be confronted with, what options the user should have to add content, comments, etc, what tasks or mini games might be included, and what constraints on interactivity should be foregrounded). I worked with the interface group while my artistic lead Jack Scott worked with the aesthetics group and my technical lead Michael Skelly worked with the interactivity group (we thought Jack was best placed to help with aesthetics and Michael would be best placed to know how feasible it was to implement ideas for interactive capacities).

Each group discussed how their element of the i-doc should be designed to best convey their shared experiences and opinions about lockdown. During the breakout groups, we used a WhatsApp group to share emerging decisions, helping to inform each other's thinking. For example, the interactivity group shared an idea members had about accessing the i-doc footage through a revolving window and this sparked an idea in the interface group about the delineation of indoor and outdoor space (which I'll talk more about shortly). We then came back into the main Zoom room, shared ideas, and worked together to assemble these into a coherent design plan. After the workshop, I wrote up this design and shared it with all participants to ensure it accurately represented their ideas. Jack and Michael used this design to produce components for the i-doc. Jack made the artistic components (soundscape, background images, icons, arrows, etc) and Michael wrote the code that would assemble these parts and allow users to move through them and interact. At the third workshop, we showed a draft of the i-doc design to the participants and they made suggestions for final edits before it was completed.

Making content for the i-doc enabled the group to express their individual experiences. Content is labelled to show who made it (using pseudonyms where participants chose to do so), allowing users to see how differently each group member approached and experienced the pandemic. For example, one clip shows someone washing shopping in the sink, while another is an extended account of attending illegal parties and defying lockdown rules. Yet, despite these extreme differences, the group were able to come to a shared agreement about what the i-doc should be like.

The group decided that the i-doc should have several pages, each showing different rooms inside a home and different spaces in a local area. They agreed that the backdrops for these spaces should be collaged together from stills from their own materials, so that it was a generic yet actual space. They decided their content should be accessed by clicking on objects in these various pages. Content is grouped thematically. For example, a yoga mat can be clicked on to see content about exercise. Each clickable object illuminates slightly when hovered over so that the user can see it has interactive features. This is the primary pathway of discovery for content within the i-doc. By 'pathway of discovery' I mean a route or mechanism through which the user is encouraged to navigate the i-doc interface and come across i-doc content.

Users can navigate the various pages of the i-doc by clicking arrows at the bottom of the screen. Occasionally, they'll be accosted by a pop-up window that asks them a question, makes a suggestion, or gives an order. For example one pop-up asks them if they've washed their hands, another if they have their mask. Others ask if they want to 'bulk buy loo roll?' or 'take a family Zoom call'. The pop-up windows are also a secondary pathway of discovery. Some pop-ups take users to collections of content. For example if a user chooses to 'play on Instagram', they're taken to a collection of content filmed in selfie mode. Some of the pop-ups are satirical. For example: 'Do you want an injection of bleach? Donald Trump thinks it's a great idea!'

As the user navigates the interface, engages with content, and responds to pop-ups, two meters in the bottom left and right corners of the screen track their well-being levels and viral-risk levels. Balancing these meters is difficult, as many of the pieces of content that raise well-being (for example, going to the park) also raise your viral risk. This gamified element reflects the group's shared experience of lockdown feeling like an unwinnable game.

One aspect of *The Lockdown Game*'s interface that I'd like to talk about is the group's decision to make a clear distinction between indoor and outdoor spaces. Within indoor and outdoor areas, respectively, the user can navigate between locations using arrows. However, to pass between the indoors and the outdoors they have to click on a door icon that's only accessible on the kitchen page of the indoor area and the garden page of the outdoor area. Indoors and outdoors are also demarcated by different soundscapes. The soundscape for indoor pages was made, by Jack, by mixing together sounds from clips and audio that participants recorded within their homes, while the outdoor soundscape was mixed from their outdoor content.

This division in the i-doc reflected participants' distinctive experience of space during lockdown. Participants spoke about the claustrophobia of being stuck indoors but also the disorientation of being outdoors, especially during the first surreal weeks of lockdown. Suddenly, the outdoors had become something semi-mysterious and off-limits while the inside of the home had become the extent of people's worlds. Participants' decision to divide indoor and outdoor spaces in the i-doc interface communicates this strange new geography. At the workshops, one participant described how 'I felt like literally my whole life was lived within this tiny space – looking out the window again.'

But, more than this, thinking through how the indoor versus outdoor interface division should work in the i-doc enabled participants to think about power and its unequal distributions. Participants arrived at the idea of structuring the interface around indoor versus outdoor spaces because they noticed that windows were a common motif in people's content. This prompted one member of the infrastructure breakout group to note that windows are important because 'a window [questions] where are you, are you looking in from the outside and trying to help, or are you inside?' Another participant riffed off this to suggest that the i-doc could open with 'two categories – inside and outdoors, and that's the beginning'. This idea for the opening didn't end up in the final design, but the discussion shows how the indoor/outdoor division was initially related to questions of who was safe indoors and who was out on the frontline. At the time this was at the forefront of the public imagination, given that key workers (including medical staff, delivery drivers, shop workers, funeral workers, etc) were allowed out to provide essential services but, in doing so, put themselves at much higher risk of contracting COVID.

This distinction between who was helping and who was being helped was problematised by the participants as the design evolved. In the main group discussion following the breakout groups, the interactivity group explained their idea of having pop-up windows that give you instructions and ask questions. One of the pop-up windows was a question that users might encounter when they try to move between indoor and outdoor spaces. The question says 'this journey is illegal, unless you're Dominic Cummings?' and gives users the option to choose 'I am' or 'I am not.'

This pop-up question is a satirical reference to the breaching of lockdown rules by the then UK Government Chief Advisor Dominic Cummings, who drove 25 miles to a tourist spot, while having suspected COVID, at a time when the vast majority of the public were under severe lockdown restrictions (because of rules he was involved in creating), unable even to see dying relatives. The decision to include this pop-up question sheds a different light on the indoor versus outdoor division and how it relates to questions of who's helping and who's being helped. While the group had initially thought about this distinction in relation to those isolating and those helping as key workers, the Dominic Cummings pop-up raises the idea that some of the people 'outdoors' were not actually helping, but instead acting as if they were exempt while imposing stay-at-home orders for others.

At the workshop, participants discussed how the 'Dominic Cummings moment' caused them to reassess the logic under which they had been living. One remembered that, while people had previously been 'questioning, is it okay to go out for two hours, if I'm only meant to go out for one?', this new knowledge of how politicians were behaving made them feel like they'd been duped by a government who thought that the public's freedoms were less valuable than the freedoms of those in charge.

I'll talk more about the satirical aspects of the i-doc and how this related to the group's analysis of lockdown in Chapter 4. For now, I just want to reiterate how designing the spatial infrastructure of the i-doc illuminated a complex power differential between those indoors and those outside.

In the three examples given in this chapter we can see how valuable i-doc design is for illuminating and articulating how power is embedded in space. The spatial configuration of power is something evident and well understood. From road markings to borders, spatial markings tell us what we can and can't do and where. However, identifying power geometries beyond these tangible markings in space can be more complex. Designing an i-doc interface can be a nuanced way to explore the power geographies of a topic. The questions listed at the start, as well as others you might come up with yourself, offer routes into questioning and defining how power is distributed, negotiated, contested, and enforced through spatialised relations.

4

Aesthetics

> **Key chapter arguments**
>
> - Designing i-doc aesthetics can help researchers to focus on dimensions of affect, mood, atmosphere, emotion, and feeling in their topics.
> - I-docs are particularly good at drawing attention to the intersection of moods and affects at different scales.

Aesthetics

The aesthetics of an i-doc are hugely important as they will change the impact of all other components. The same interactive capacities or temporal architectures can have very different affects simply by changing fonts, colour schemes, or soundscapes. Designing i-doc aesthetics helps to think through multiple aspects of research topics, but, in particular, demands attention to mood, atmosphere, emotion, and feeling. In this chapter we'll explore how designing i-doc aesthetics helps to elucidate these often intangible qualities of research subjects. But we'll also go a step further. The main capacity I want to highlight (of i-doc aesthetic design as a mode of encountering the world) is the capacity to elucidate how *localised* moods and affects connect to more *pervasive* structures of feeling. This argument progresses work I have undertaken elsewhere

Table 4.1: Key terms

Key terms	
Localised affects *Inspired by Ben* *Anderson (2014)*	The affective atmospheres present in specific areas of an i-doc. For example, a video included in an i-doc might have a hopeful affective atmosphere even though the i-doc as a whole is morose. Or one page in an i-doc might have an ominous affective atmosphere that isn't apparent in the other pages. This term builds on Ben Anderson's work on affect.
Pervasive affects *Inspired by Ben* *Anderson (2014)*	The affective atmospheres that pervade an i-doc. For example, the affective atmosphere that dominates the experience of engaging with the i-doc, based on its aesthetics and other components. Again, this builds on Anderson's work.
Invited mode of spectatorship *My invention*	The particular conventions of encounter that a user is invited to bring to an i-doc. For example, are they invited to view it in a mode of play, a mode of discovery, a mode of concern, and so on? The invitation will be crafted subtly by the aesthetics and discourses of the i-doc and sometimes explicitly by introductory text or an introductory clip that frames the i-doc experience and sets up expectations for how to engage.
Foregrounding device *My invention*	An element of an i-doc that foregrounds particular parts or meanings of a topic. For example, a childish aesthetic in an i-doc about life in a refugee camp would foreground children's experiences.
Orientation device *My invention*	Elements like arrows, maps, instructions, and so on that guide the audience's engagement with the i-doc.

that develops a nuanced analysis of interactions between affect at the level of the individual, localised affective atmospheres, and collective feelings at a wider scale (Harris, 2019).

Social science researchers have explored mood and affect at national scales (Forket, 2017; Highmore, 2017; Davies, 2018) and local scales (Anderson, 2009; Shaw & Warf, 2009; Churcher et al, 2023). Some thinkers have also examined the interactions between affects at different scales, including Sara Ahmed's investigation of how national moods require the affective alienation of specific individuals (Ahmed, 2014) and Lauren Berlant's influential work on affect as a personal and political device. In this chapter I suggest that designing the aesthetics of i-docs can further this crucial work of understanding entanglements of moods and affects at different scales.

This chapter's discussions will mostly focus around the two biggest i-doc projects I've worked on myself: *The Lockdown Game* and *The Temporary City*. Through a detailed discussion of the design process, I'll explore how designing the aesthetics of *The Temporary City* refined my analysis of how the local affective atmospheres of pop-up places (which are exciting and quasi-subversive), rebrand a broader structure of feeling in the post-2008 city (of precarity). I'll also show how creating the aesthetics of *The Lockdown Game* defined a tension my participants experienced during lockdown between an atmosphere of 'being playful' (in the diversions they created for themselves and their young children) and a wider feeling of 'being played' by the UK government.

As I'm sure you can imagine, i-doc aesthetics are incredibly varied. Like other elements of i-docs, they are used to communicate and critique the subjects explored. For example in *Highrise: The Universe Within*, an i-doc about the digital lives of high-rise residents, discernibly pixelated images are used to evoke the feel of digital space. Rather than use a static image as its backdrop, the main page of the i-doc presents a 3D image that moves with the cursor, immersing the user in a digital environment. Conversely, the i-doc *Migrant Mothers of Syria* uses handwriting-style fonts and a background that looks like crumpled paper to immediately create a homely, family feel. Each clip is linked to a fragment of a drawing of a family home, ripped at the edges. *Migrant Mothers of Syria* uses this aesthetic to foreground the humanity of migrant mothers, emphasising their day-to-day family life rather than focusing on geopolitical dimensions of forced migration.

I-doc aesthetics are very useful as a foregrounding device. Aesthetic elements can help to foreground particular aspects of your topic as well as help to bring particular sections or functions of your i-doc front and centre. For example, in some i-docs, the interface itself is very attentively designed (as, for example, with the hand-drawn maps of *Refugee Republic* we explored in Chapter 3). In these instances, the user is invited to pay as much attention to the interface as to the pieces of content embedded in it. Other i-docs, however, use minimalist styles in the interface itself so that the submitted content takes centre stage. *Corona Haikus* presents a wall of submitted images from the COVID-19 lockdown period, which, when clicked, are displayed on a white background alongside poems that accompany the images and some sparse explanatory text. The 'neutrality' (if there is such a thing) of the interface encourages users to see it as just a backdrop for the submitted content.

I-docs can also use their aesthetics to signal that particular modes of consumption/spectatorship are invited. I-docs that begin with cinematic film sequences invite a cinematic mode of spectatorship that users will be familiar with from feature films and traditional documentary. I-docs that provide little orientation or signposting but lead with soundscapes and creative visuals invite a more conceptual mode of spectatorship, more like that required in an art gallery. Others present in ways that demand a mode of consumption akin to traditional journalism. For example *Seven Deadly Digital Sins*, an i-doc made in collaboration between the National Film Board of Canada and the *Guardian* newspaper, uses traditional journalistic talking head clips, as well as graphs and charts, amidst its content to signal a journalistic authority.

The aesthetics of an i-doc obviously have a huge impact on the kind of feelings a user might have in response to an i-doc. Scholarship on aesthetics and affect has explored how affect theory can make sense of the influence that aesthetic forms can have on our personal and collective feelings (O'Sullivan, 2001; Ioanes, 2017). Affect theory can account for how aesthetic elements of texts, music, pictures, and so on do more than just communicate feelings as semantic signifiers, but actively evoke feelings in us. Designing aesthetic elements of i-docs is, then, crucial in generating the emotional experience that the i-doc creates. And that emotional experience is key to how the user will respond to the i-doc.

So, what kind of questions does the design of i-doc aesthetics require?

Box 4.1: Ideation notes for aesthetics

- What is the mood/ feel that's appropriate to create for this i-doc? Should it be playful? Scary? Dramatic? Surreal? To create this mood/these moods, what are the appropriate choices of:
  - fonts
  - colour schemes
  - icons
  - soundscape(s)
  - sound effects
  - styles of arrows and other orientation devices?
- How much movement should there be on the screen to create the right feel in your i-doc? Consider how surreal or lucid you want it to be. Do you want a static image as the backdrop, a video clip, or a backdrop with subtle movement?
- With what mode of spectatorship do you want your audience to approach the i-doc? As an experiment? As a creative work? As a journalistic piece? As a direct encounter with your participants? What kind of aesthetic choices will signal this? What are the appropriate choices in relation to:
  - amount of explanatory text
  - signposting/nudging for how to use the i-doc
  - information about the project?

  You might also want to reconsider all the things in this list (fonts, colour scheme, soundscape, sound effects, arrows, and orientation devices) with this in mind.
- Should there be variations in different aspects and elements of your i-doc. For example: Should pieces of content have different moods/feels/atmospheres to the interface? Should there be different pages or segments with different atmospheres? Should there be a shift at a temporal point where the mood/atmosphere changes? And so on.

Answering these questions will start to flesh out the aesthetic design of your i-doc and help to think about how different moods and atmospheres at different scales interact within your research topic. Equally, as we'll see, these questions can be a way into illuminating conceptual issues too.

The Temporary City

I've already introduced *The Temporary City*, so if you're reading this book non-linearly I'd recommend going to Chapter 2 to learn what it's about and how I made it. Here I'm going to focus on its aesthetic dimensions and how designing those helped me to think about the interaction of affects at different scales: pervasive structures of feeling and localised affective atmospheres. As I'll show, aesthetics design both illuminated the interscalar function of affects within pop-up culture *and* helped me to understand affect better as a concept; principally, that there is a need to attend to how affects at different scales intersect.

If you're not familiar with work around affect then 'affective atmospheres' is a term used to note the 'particular feel' or 'tone' of 'sites, episodes or encounters' (Anderson, 2014, 138). Ben Anderson has explored affective atmospheres in his excellent work on affect theory. He describes how affective atmospheres are collectively felt by groups of people but also impact on each individual in unique ways. Affective atmospheres are what give situations their 'charge' (Anderson, 2014, 139). We've all had the experience of being swept away by the atmosphere of a nightclub, a protest, or a sports event. As Anderson explains, charges can be political and politicised, as in the atmosphere of hope at the inauguration of Barack Obama (Anderson, 2014, 2).

While affective atmospheres describe relatively contained collective feelings (contained to an event with reasonably clear temporal and spatial boundaries), other terms have been used by theorists to explore longer term, more spatially dispersed, and (therefore?) more nebulous collective experiences. Perhaps most famously, cultural critic Raymond Williams has described how moments in social history have distinctive 'structures of feeling', a term he uses to encapsulate the felt experience of meanings and values emerging in a particular socio-historical setting (Williams, 2011, 133). While multiple structures of feeling can be present in any given place and time, and while they can be experienced differently by different groups, these collective feelings are much more pervasive than affective atmospheres; they belong to a chapter of history, rather than to a particular event. Anderson elucidates the distinction further, suggesting that structures of feeling set 'limits' and exert 'pressure', providing the parameters within which day-to-day life is experienced and unfolds, while an affective atmosphere 'surrounds' and 'envelopes', impacting emotions and behaviours within the intensities of a scene.

In my writing about pop-up culture, I've argued that pop-up is instrumental within a structure of feeling of precarity that was dominant in the UK in the aftermath of the 2008 financial crash. For me, this structure of feeling was pervasive until roughly 2016, after which point events, including the Brexit vote and the COVID-19 crisis, saw a different structure of feeling emerge, one I'd argue was defined by absurdity (but that's for another book!). Others have also argued for precarity as a definitive structure of feeling post the 2008 crash (Berlant, 2011; Anderson, 2014) as well as for austerity as a 'public mood' in the same period (Forkert, 2017).

As I've explained in previous chapters, my work on pop-up argues that pop-up culture is a result of precarity (responding to a sudden increase of vacant shops and spaces, as well as to cuts in funding for charities, the arts, and small businesses) as well as a mechanism by which precarity was normalised. However, pop-up places like the ones I studied for my PhD aren't themselves dominated by moods of precarity but instead by moods of excitement and intrigue (there certainly are some pop-up spaces, like pop-up hospitals, courts, legal services, etc that feel very precarious indeed, but I was focusing on pop-up spaces of leisure and consumption).

I-doc making assisted me in thinking through how pop-ups' localised atmospheres of excitement and intrigue are entangled with the broader structure of feeling of precarity. It helped me to craft my argument that pop-up culture normalises precarity by stopping us from feeling that precarity, which it does by reimagining symptoms of precarity so they can be experienced positively. For example, pop-up reimagines instability in urban spaces as 'flexibility', uncertainty about the future as 'surprise', and diminishing space standards in housing as the cachet of quirky 'micro' homes.

So how did aesthetic design in my i-doc enable me to explore this process of rebranding precarity? As I've already described in Chapter 2, designing the temporal architecture of *The Temporary City* helped me to articulate pop-up's affective atmospheres. The calendar at the bottom of the screen and clips that come and go conjure the dynamism and unpredictability of pop-up while clicking on the icons to reveal clips indicates secrecy. The aesthetics of the interface were also key to this atmosphere. I say *were* because sadly the aesthetic overlay we used for the map no longer works as the application (something called Snazzy Maps) is now defunct. When it was functioning, it provided a colour scheme that connoted a stylish and fashionable urban phenomenon: a darkened map with semi-fluorescent road markings and bright fluorescent icons dotted across it. The aesthetics of the entry page were also key to this aesthetic. Dark colours, a typewriter-style font, and a hard-to-make-out but intriguing image immediately invite the user into an immersive mode of spectatorship. The text on this page loads bit by bit, like movie titles, enhancing that cinematic feel. These aesthetic decisions were crucial in helping me to articulate the defining features of affective atmospheres within pop-up culture, including their immersiveness and their encouragement for visitors to explore with an attitude of 'serious play'.

The aesthetic decisions I made when creating the contents of the i-docs – its film clips and collaged images – were also part of articulating pop-up's affective atmospheres. For example, one clip is about 'Pulp Kitchen', an immersive screening of the film *Pulp Fiction*, named as such because spectators were given snacks and drinks at various points in the film that were related to the on-screen action. For example, at the famous scene in *Pulp Fiction* where the character Mia is given an adrenaline shot following an accidental overdose, the audience were given a shot of alcohol in a syringe. When I edited the clip, I tried to capture the affective atmosphere of this screening: the embodied immersion of the audience within an extended filmic world. I did this by juxtaposing still images of the food and drinks given to guests with their on-screen correlates. I added gunshot sounds to announce the arrival of each image, giving it a *Pulp Fiction* feel. In this way, the clip I produced connected the off-screen and the on-screen elements, just as the event created this extended filmic atmosphere.

The dominant aesthetic in *The Temporary City* is the aesthetic I think evokes pop-up's affective atmospheres. It reflects pop-up's self-representation as a cool, urban phenomenon. However, there's one element of the i-doc for which I designed a different aesthetic: the 'outside pop-up city' pages. In Chapter 2, I discussed how the outside pop-up city pages helped me to critique the pop-up's non-linear temporal imaginaries. Here, I'm going to focus on their aesthetic design and the role of this aesthetic in articulating how pop-up's affective atmospheres transmute precarity as a structure of feeling so that it is not felt as acutely. The outside pop-up city pages are collages I made on Photoshop. They are deliberately rough, splicing together discordant images. In contrast to the sleek fluorescent icons and dark colour scheme of the map interface, their colours are muted and the images often grainy. This juxtaposing aesthetic helps to signal that the pop-up city pages reveal something that doesn't feature in pop-up's self-representation.

For example, one clip in the i-doc is about a supper club called 'The Ship's Kitchen'. This was a supper club held on a houseboat moored in Barking, East London. The houseboat location was marketed as a selling point for the supper club. As with the clip about Pulp Kitchen, I edited this clip to evoke its affective atmosphere. As the clip begins the camera rolls rapidly towards the door of the barge while a drum roll progresses (which we'll soon learn is the sound of live music being played by a two-man band inside). This shot ends as my hand emerges from behind the camera to open the door. This dramatised opening evokes the affective atmosphere of secrecy and surprise cultivated in this and other supper clubs.

The outside pop-up city page offered as an option at the end of this clip, however, provides a different perspective. The collage in the box is created using images from the New London Architecture catalogue that year and shows designs that purport to alleviate the housing crisis in London by 'colonising' the waterways with 'waterhoods'; floating houses that will turn 'generation rent' into 'generation float'. Two different architectural plans are spliced together: one a map of a proposed '34th Borough' in the Thames Estuary and the other images of floating houses. Everything in the collage is at a jaunty angle – an aesthetic indication that this is an alternative perspective. In the top right part of the image there is a black slash through the white canvas. This punky aesthetic suggests that the information given is an intervention from outside the dominant narrative. At the top of the image the text reads 'The housing crisis is pushing increasing numbers of young Londoners onto the waterways.'

The outside pop-up city page sheds a new light on the location of The Ship's Kitchen supper club. As well as a quirky destination for a dining event, this boat is evidence of young people ending up in 'compensatory' (Harris, 2019) forms of housing at a time of intense housing precarity. It is in these instances, then, that localised affective atmospheres and pervasive structures of feeling come into contact via pop-up. Housing insecurity was (and remains) a significant element of precarity as a structure of feeling in the period issuing from the 2008 financial crash. Yet the affective atmosphere of The Ship's Kitchen repels this structure of feeling of precarity, instead presenting the location as having cachet. The localised atmosphere of secrecy and surprise offers an experience that mutates what would otherwise be felt as housing precarity, instead presenting the barge as an exciting and unusual location.

I hope this example shows how designing contrasting aesthetic elements of the i-doc helped me to articulate how affective atmospheres can dilute and transmute structures of feeling. I was able to identify how pop-up's affective atmospheres transform precarity as a structure of feeling so that certain aspects of urban precarity are not felt as such, but instead are normalised and glamorised. I was also able to make a conceptual breakthrough in my work – identifying how affects at different scales intersect in ways that do not always reinforce each other but sometimes transform each other. This way of encountering the world – this attunement to affects at different scales – is afforded by the specificities of i-docs as a medium. As we've seen through the examples in this book, i-docs typically organise multiple discrete pieces of content within an interface. This means they are formally predicated on how localised instances relate to a generalised picture. Making an i-doc, then, requires attention to what those relationships between pieces of content and a wider interface should be and why. This process refines our thinking about how localised atmospheres relate to wider structures of feeling.

Being playful

The aesthetic design of *The Lockdown Game* also illuminated interactions between moods and feelings at different scales.

Aesthetics

For those reading non-sequentially, Chapter 3 introduces *The Lockdown Game* and the participatory process of its making.

At our i-doc-making workshop, the breakout group responsible for aesthetics made the key decisions that created the feel and mood of *The Lockdown Game*. They decided that the i-doc should open with a 'confusing cacophony' (as one participant put it) of news statements about lockdown, to reflect the disorientation at the beginning of the pandemic. But they thought that, after this confusing cacophony, the i-doc should then become playful and personal because, despite the gravity of the situation, play had been central to their experiences of life during lockdown. The group noted that there was a 'homemade kind of look' in the pieces of content people had submitted to the i-doc that reflected the ways in which they had found themselves inventing playful and ad hoc ways to make their day-to-day routines liveable.

To achieve the playful aesthetic the group decided on handwriting-style fonts and a scrapbook style for orientation devices (arrows, buttons, etc), including torn edges on labels and hand-drawn arrows. To convey the personal feel, they agreed that the backdrop images for each room/outdoor area in the i-doc, as well as the border around the main screen, would be made by collaging images taken from the content that each of them had made. They wanted to make sure that visual signifiers of the pandemic were pervasive, but agreed that this could be done by incorporating images from people's content – much of which included images of masks, social-distancing signs, visiting neighbours at their window, and so on. The group also decided to create soundscapes, again by collaging together noises from the groups' content. They wanted a separate soundscape for the indoor and the outdoor areas, to reflect the eeriness of venturing outside during lockdown.

When the aesthetics breakout group presented their proposal to the main group, there was widespread agreement that a playful aesthetic would work well, but some group members did voice concerns about that style detracting from the tragedies of the pandemic and alienating users who had had terrible experiences. After much discussion, the group as a whole arrived at a solution, which was to embed links in the i-doc that signpost users to support groups, protest movements, helplines, and so on.

It's important to note that the decisions made about aesthetics, although agreed by the group as a whole, came from specific people in this breakout group. Two out of three of them were parents to young children, which probably influenced their perspective. In one of the one-to-one interviews I held at the end of the project, another participant who didn't have children (Sarah, a young woman living with her parents) – noted that:

> Everyone seemed so positive ... there were quite a few families and young families ... a lot of them were in that family unit ... if you don't have kids you don't have to make it into a fun experience ... I had different frustrations ...[I] had a different kind of lockdown.

Clearly, when co-designing an interactive documentary, group decisions won't always reflect the perspectives of all members equally. Indeed, quieter people, or people who aren't able to attend all meetings (Sarah was absent from the breakout group half of the key design workshop), won't necessarily be able to voice objections. I think the playful mood of the i-doc probably did directly relate to the fact that most participants in the aesthetics group were parents and had used play and games to try and keep the situation hopeful.

Reflecting on the play theme, one father in the group, Brian, compared the task of keeping home life positive during the pandemic to the film *Life is Beautiful*, which is set in a concentration camp where a father tries to narrate the experience to his young son as if it's a game, as the only way he knows to make it bearable. This comparison was interesting in relation to the playful design of the i-doc, suggesting that the playful mood the group decided on (Brian wasn't in the aesthetics breakout group but agreed that the play theme resonated with him) was rooted in this experience of trying to make light of a disorientating and scary situation.

In the content submitted by participants we see many instances of play and games. For example, Johanna submitted a video of herself and her daughter skateboarding into towers made of loo roll – making light of the loo roll shortages that stemmed from panic buying in the early stages of the pandemic. Beth's content explains how she made up games for her children with the limited resources they had, finding pleasure in small goals like trying to find a ladybird every day. We also see Sylvia creating Easter egg hunts inside her flat for her young child, and Megan creating elaborate dens in her parents' garden for her young toddler.

Although Sarah said the playful spirit exhibited by other participants was a long way from her experience, some of the other non-parents in the group had their own versions of games to make lockdown bearable. For example, Olga submitted content about her resurgence of interest in tarot card readings during the pandemic, suggesting a different kind of play – a play designed to experiment and explore ideas at a time when so much was up in the air. Equally, Nuria's submission of extensive maps of her lockdown walks and the different recipes she tried cooking each night are also evidence of attempts to make life in lockdown meaningful by introducing playful challenges and experiments.

The necessity of games in making meaning is something that Existentialist philosophers and associated writers knew well. Albert Camus, for example, has discussed this in his writing about football. As a teenager Camus was a keen footballer and he was vocal about how his love of football informed his philosophy. It taught him that all human games (be they sports, politics, work, art, etc) are, fundamentally, as ridiculous as getting a ball over a line. But, crucially, he knew that this inherent meaninglessness doesn't mean that games aren't also the primary space in which we *create* meaning and value. Just as football is fundamentally meaningless but becomes the basis for so much investment of hope, collaboration, conflict, despair, and so on, life is made up of games that, despite their absurdity, give us a platform for meaning creation.

Camus learnt this lesson painfully when his footballing career was cut short by tuberculosis. Being torn from the game he loved showed him the contingency, as well as the power, of all meaning-making systems. I'd say it's no coincidence that Camus explored this idea in his novel *The Plague*, and that my participants arrived at a similar conception when experiencing their own plague. Pandemics interrupt the games that normally make life meaningful – the routines of work, leisure, culture, and so on.

The void that this interruption creates reminds us that it is those games that give us a sense of purpose.

Other Existentialists, including De Beauvoir and Sartre, wrote about the nausea that ensues when we realise that the games we've lived our lives by are just made up – contingent structures that can easily be taken away. I'd argue that lockdown prompted this realisation for many people, and certainly for my participants. As lockdown was enforced so suddenly, overnight, they realised that the patternings of life that seem so stable can be interrupted and reimagined at any time. It was this nausea from which they tried to shield their children, by replacing the normal games of life with other games, to reinstate meaning and structure.

Designing the aesthetics of *The Lockdown Game*, then, helped the group to arrive at an evaluation of lockdown as a time when an unprecedented (in their lives) interruption of routines, cultures, and systems left a void within which play was crucial to getting by and to keeping life meaningful.

Being played

However, the playful mood of the i-doc takes on a different tone in other dimensions of the interface. Departing from the childlike play of the scrapbook aesthetic, other elements are playful in a way that is much more aligned with satire or parody.

During the workshops, the group defined a shared experience of what you could call *being played* by the UK government during lockdown. They broadly felt that lockdown rules had been absurd: nonsensical, impossible to follow, and not designed for the good of the people.

This extract from a conversation at the design workshop shows the group beginning to arrive at this critique.

Brian: There could be a health indicator as to how healthy things you're doing are ... mental health and physical health ... a risk-level meter

Beth: If you click on something you might find interesting but that isn't allowed ... like shopping ... anything group wise, or activism ... you're more at risk ...

Aesthetics

	but if you click on a Zoom call you're less at risk ... you get points or something
Sylvia:	Maybe when you go to the pub you get the virus
Brian:	This sounds like a game or something now ...

Based on the discussion (of which this extract is a part), the group decided that the i-doc should feel like an unwinnable game. They felt that this would reflect their experience of trying to follow lockdown rules.

As I introduced in Chapter 2, one of the interactive features of *The Lockdown Game* is pop-up windows that appear every so often, asking users satirical questions. We'll discuss these more in the next chapter, but for now I just want to note how their design adds to this satirical critique of lockdown as an unwinnable game. The questions asked in these pop-up boxes are sometimes sensible, for example, 'Have you got your mask?' but at other times a clear satire, for example, 'This journey is illegal. Unless you're Dominic Cummings?'

The group decided that the pop-up boxes should look like the pop-up adverts you would get in the early days of the internet. Those of us old enough will remember the irritating boxes that would pop-up with questions or statements, often generating a seemingly infinite stream of additional boxes when you tried to click out of them. The design of the pop-up boxes in the i-doc harks back to this frustrating experience and amplifies the satire, conveying the frustrating and bewildering array of instructions thrown at people during lockdown.

Other design elements extended this satirical critique. The meter that Brian suggests in the extract ended up being a key design feature and became central to the game-like feel. In the final design there are two meters that measure your viral risk and well-being as you move through the interface and engage with content. The group designed the viral-risk meter as an imitation of the Nando's 'PERi-PERi meter' (a pepper-shaped thermometer that measures the spiciness of chicken at Nando's chain restaurants, to which, as many commentators pointed out, the government's own initial risk-level meter looked suspiciously similar). The cool/green end of the meter indicates that you're currently at low risk of catching coronavirus while the hot/dark-red end suggests your imminent contamination. The other meter the group chose to include is a 'well-being' meter, depicted by a hand-drawn rainbow like those stuck on the insides of windows during the lockdown to thank the NHS and key workers and encourage positivity. The rainbow is colourless when your well-being is low, but fills up clockwise if your well-being rises.

These two meters are playful in their aesthetics and also in their function. They 'gamify' the i-doc by suggesting that it is hypothetically possible to win or lose, or at least to do better or worse based on the way you 'play' with the i-doc. As you move through its contents, your well-being and viral risk go up and down, encouraging you to think about the consequences of your choices within it. The meters also invite a particular mode of spectatorship. They suggest that the visitor to the i-doc has a personalised presence, like a player. While the i-doc's contents are the same for any visitor, the meters change according to each person's own particular actions; emphasising that each person is an individual within it and that their navigations of that content have ramifications for them personally.

In the design workshop, Brian described the kind of decisions people had to make in real life when balancing the risk of the virus with the threat to their mental health:

> [It was the] everyday decisions that we made ... do you want to go to the corner shop? How much do you need that chocolate bar? You might get coronavirus and die but you might have some chocolate ... everything was a risk assessment ... our own personal risk assessment. ... Do you hug your gran? Would she feel amazing if you did that but you might kill her?

It's interesting that Brian used the term 'personal risk assessment'. I don't think it indicates that Brian was only thinking about himself. His weighing up of whether people should be hugging their grans or not shows his concern about collective well-being as well as his own. I use the term in the sense that Brian sees negotiating viral and well-being risks as something that needed to be based on one's own judgement of the collective good despite the fact that, in theory, national guidelines were in place that were intended (at least ostensibly) to determine precisely what was in the collective good. This reveals why lockdown felt like, and was therefore represented by the participants as, a game. Following instructions uncritically isn't a game, it's a process. But navigating instructions becomes game-like when those instructions are an oblique framework within which you need to make your own decisions without being able to fully predict the outcome.

The meters, then, express the game-like experience of trying to navigate lockdown rules. But as you progress through the i-doc it becomes clear quite quickly that this is not a winnable game. As we'll discuss more in Chapter 5, the meters are often in conflict, because things that increase your viral risk might also improve your well-being, for example watching a video about a house party might increase both viral risk and well-being. Choosing not to go out into the street might improve your viral-risk levels but also negatively impact your well-being meter.

As one participant, Beth, put it:

> [W]e're playing around with the can't win situation … whether you're trying to do something well or you don't bother at all you can't really win … cause what's greater, the impact of not seeing anyone or the impact of corona?

Beth even suggested that the best way to convey the experience of lockdown would be that, rather than logical well-being and viral-risk points being given to pieces of content, it could be 'a completely arbitrary scale' so that that 'actually everything's totally random … so you think you're doing something healthy but it's not … the more you try to do something it's actually by the by anyway'.

Beth's suggestion resonated with the group who'd all experienced frustration at the conflicting and ever-changing governmental advice about what was and wasn't safe. They shared stories about friends and neighbours who, in the hysteria of early lockdown, had taken up clearly ridiculous instructions like 'washing your vegetables in bleach' and recalled how early instruction from central government, for example that masks weren't necessary, had been completely contradicted by later advice and legislation.

Amidst the absurdity of formal and informal advice they felt it was impossible to know the right ways to do things and foolish to take any guidelines at face value.

For Beth, the i-doc reflected the impossibility of winning lockdown itself.

> [I]t plays on the ... it kind of simulates the kind of people who just play on the website and don't give a toss about this random scale in the background, and those who are actively trying to keep it low, and those who are stumbling along realising things have gone wrong so try to reverse and change it. ... It's so changeable that it can never really be right.

The sense of absurdity generated by these meters is amplified by their design. The playful and comic aesthetics of the sunshine/rainbow well-being meter and PERi-PERi spice-level viral-risk meter defy the user to take the balancing act seriously. Then, when you add in the frustrating design of the pop-up windows (making suggestions like 'Do you want an injection of bleach to cure COVID? Donald Trump thinks it's a great idea!' or 'This journey is illegal. Unless you're Dominic Cummings?'), the user begins to get the sense that, in trying to follow these rules, they are not so much playing as *being played*.

As in *The Temporary City*, the aesthetic design of different elements of *The Lockdown Game* creates an analysis of how localised moods and feelings intersect with affects at a wider scale. Here, it shows how the playful spirit of coping strategies on a domestic level sat against, and for many gradually dissipated into, a feeling of being played by lockdown rules that were impossible to follow and not honoured by the people enforcing them. I think this is a fantastic example of how a nuanced analysis of a research topic can arise from participatory i-doc making. This conceptualisation of lockdown's localised affects and pervasive affects was produced collectively through the process of i-doc making. I was then able to refine its expression in my retrospective analysis of the i-doc and its making.

5

Interactivity

> **Key chapter arguments**
>
> - Designing interactive capacities (and lacks of them) in i-docs can focus attention on issues of freedom and compliance.
>
> - Interactive capacities in i-docs can invite both researchers and audiences to consider their own complicity and agency.

Interactivity, freedom, compliance

Interactivity (and its absence) is a huge topic to cover when thinking about i-docs as methods. Interactivity is a defining feature of i-docs and is part of how other i-doc elements, like those we've already explored (spatial infrastructure, temporal architecture, aesthetics) take shape and generate meaning. Here I'm going to focus on one key mode of encounter that designing interactive capacities of i-docs engages: attention to freedom and compliance.

Theorists have written a lot about how i-docs cultivate attention to agency. I-docs require user interaction to function. Nothing will happen if audiences don't click. Many i-doc makers deliberately mobilise this requirement to foreground the power to make change in relation to documentary issues. In this chapter

Table 5.1: Key terms

Key terms	
Call to action *Borrowed from marketing terminology*	Call to action is a term used a lot in communications and marketing strategies. It refers to an invitation made to an audience to *do* something based on the information/media you're presenting them with. In a blog post, the call to action might be to sign up to an event. In i-docs there are often calls to action presented to audiences, including invitations to follow links, submit content, leave feedback, and so on, but also more indirect calls to action, such as to change behaviour in relation to social or political challenges.
Agency frustration *My invention derived from participants*	The ways in which a user's choices are frustrated within i-docs, through limitations on what they can do and when. For example, there might be content that you can't watch until you've completed a particular task, or time limits on how long you can stay within certain parts of the i-doc.
Complicity Compulsion *My invention*	I was inspired to invent this term by the German word 'zugzwang', which means 'compulsion to move'. *Zugzwang* refers to situations in turn-based games (like chess) where you *have* to move but any move available to you will make your situation worse. Inspired by this, I use the term 'complicity compulsion' to describe situations in i-docs where you have to click on something, choose an option, and so on, but whatever you do will make you complicit in something you don't want to be complicit in. We'll see some examples in this chapter.
UX A common term in web design, my use of it here is inspired by Michael Skelly (my technical lead).	UX or 'user experience' refers to how a user interacts with and experiences something. As Michael Skelly explains in the section he's contributed, i-docs have a unique approach to UX. In a normal website, the aim is for users to be able to navigate so seamlessly that they don't even pay attention to interactive functions/lack of interactive functions. But in i-docs, the UX is significant in generating meaning. We want users to notice the i-doc's interactive functions because they are key to what the i-doc is conveying.

I want to shift the focus from *agency* onto the slightly different framing of *freedom and compliance*. This related but different angle hasn't been extensively discussed, even though, in my opinion, attention to tension between freedom and compliance is one of the most interesting modes of encounter that i-docs offer.

Recently, there have been a string of high-profile books on freedom, including Olivia Laing's *Everybody* (Laing, 2021), De Dijn's *Freedom: An Unruly History* (Dijn, 2020), Maggie Nelson's *On Freedom* (Nelson, 2022), and Lea Ypi's *Free: Coming of Age at the End of History* (Ypi, 2021). I think this renewed interest in freedom relates to an important shift in structures of feeling resulting from the COVID-19 pandemic. The pandemic led to restrictions on public and personal freedoms at an unprecedented scale and raised difficult questions of how to balance freedoms *from* (eg from being infected with COVID) and freedoms *to* (eg be mobile, see loved ones). I also think this increased interest in freedom relates to political shifts towards populism around the globe, which have shaken the long-standing association of freedom with dispassionate rationality and democratic process, shifting emphasis instead onto the relationships between freedom, feeling, and identity (Davies, 2018). In this context, new questions are asked about what it means to be free, which freedoms deserve safeguarding, and what it means to be complicit in the unfreedoms of others.

Despite this rising interest in freedom in contemporary non-fiction, detailed examinations of how freedom is experienced and imagined by different groups hasn't been a major focus for recent research. I argue that i-docs can give researchers detailed insights into imaginaries and experiences of freedom and compliance that are crucial for supporting nuanced debate about freedom in the new global context.

Predominantly, I'll return to *The Lockdown Game* again to discuss how we can encounter imaginaries of freedom and compliance through i-docs. In co-creating this i-doc, my participants constructed a powerful analysis of how lockdown had changed their experiences and understandings of freedom. I'll show how the process of co-designing interactive capacities enabled this.

I'll also briefly discuss a couple of other i-docs in this chapter to highlight an element of freedom and compliance that *The*

Lockdown Game doesn't foreground but which I think is important and generative in many other i-docs. This is the ability of i-docs to focus attention on freedom and compliance in digital space. As we'll see, there have been several i-docs that use their digital platforms to raise questions of what it means to be free in digital spaces, and how easily, and unwittingly, we can give up those freedoms.

Before I delve into the chapter's main discussion about i-docs and freedom it's helpful to spend a bit of time exploring arguments that have been made about the capacities of i-docs to highlight agency and to relate these to questions of method.

Lots of media theorists have argued that it is interactivity that gives i-docs their exciting political potential as a media form. Interactivity allows i-docs to confront users with their own capacity for action within whatever issue is being explored. I-docs move away from a passive model of spectatorship, because watching requires decision making. Adrian Miles has defined the scheme of engagement in i-docs as 'notice – decide – do' (Miles, 2014, 79).

Many i-docs try to channel this 'notice – decide – do' schema towards action in the 'real' world, beyond the confines of the i-doc itself. For example, as discussed by Paolo Favero, the i-doc *The Thousandth Tower*, which is part of the 'Highrise' project, prompted action in relation to the well-being of high-rise residents, including local interventions and policy changes (Cizek & Uricchio, 2022, 16).

Often i-docs make the leap between 'reel and real' by incorporating comment functions or discussion forums, encouraging users to consider and share their own views as a starting point for action. *Prison Valley* was a (no longer functional) i-doc that explored a prison town in Colorado. It had a particularly strong emphasis on user agency. Playing on ideas of truth, reality, and justice, *Prison Valley* asked users to create an avatar through which to play the role of detective within the i-doc world. As you watched clips you were able to unlock clues like photographs, extra footage, and notes. These allowed you to piece together what life is like in Prison Valley. As you met characters in the i-doc you were given the option to contact them in real life, including sending messages to some of the people in prison. Links were also offered to other relevant websites, encouraging you to pursue your own investigation of the prison industrial complex.

In *Prison Valley* the call to action was explicit. Users were invited to become active investigators of the injustices of the prison industry. In other i-docs, this call to action is more subtle. For example, in the i-doc *Migrant Mothers of Syria*, clips are accessed by clicking on images that look like torn parts of a child's drawing of a family home. Once you've watched a clip, the torn part of the picture linked to it snaps into place so that eventually, once you've watched all the clips, the child's drawing is reassembled in full. This interactive design foregrounds the user's agency in a more subtle way than in *Prison Valley*. Metaphorically, the fact that the attention you pay to the videos works to reassemble the picture suggests that your attention to this issue can help to restore hope for migrant mothers and their families. The motivation to assist that this feature aims to cultivate can then be acted on via a 'how to help' tab offered alongside the main i-doc pages. The how-to-help page offers information about charities that support the cause and links to donate.

The way i-docs invite users to consider their own potential actions within documentary topics is interesting when put in proximity to arguments about 'messy methods' (Law, 2004). In his influential work, John Law has highlighted how, in opposition to the fallacy that research can be objective and detached from the social world, methods are messy. Researchers inevitably intervene in and end up entangled with the subjects we explore. I-docs highlight this inextricable involvement. When used as methods, they can show not only how researchers are entangled with their subjects but can also demonstrate to audiences of research that they too are implicated in the subjects covered.

However, it's not just interactive capacities and their calls to action that are important in cultivating attention to freedom. Frustration of agency, though much less often discussed, is just as important an element in the modes of encounter that i-docs offer. As non-linear medium, i-docs are associated with openness and potential, but they are at least equally structured by fixity: by what *isn't* interactive. Writing about video games, James Ash has argued that a primary requirement of video-game interfaces is that contingency be rendered visible (Ash, 2009, 662) so that users know what choices are available. I'd add to this that *lack* of contingency must also be rendered visible to foreground the limits of freedom within media worlds.

Frustration of agency can come in many forms in i-docs. For example, in Chapter 2 I discussed how in my i-doc *The Temporary City* users are unable to watch all the clips in one sitting and are kicked out of the i-doc before they may be ready to leave. These frustrations are key to how meaning is created (in that instance, key to my critique of pop-up's politics.) This is an example of why it's important to consider limitations on interactivity, as well as interactive capacities, when creating an i-doc design that reflects your research topic.

Related to frustrations of agency, I think the term 'complicity compulsion' can be helpful in explaining how lack of agency is sometimes used in i-docs to foreground ethical complicity. In Chapter 2, we saw how fixed elements of the i-doc *Gaza Sderot* (such as the line down the middle) draw attention to the heavy weight of the occupation and the lack of freedom it inflicts. O'Flynn, writing about this i-doc, has suggested that the line forces the user to be complicit with the power dynamics of the occupation because to interact with the interface at all is to 'choose a side' by picking a clip from either side of the line. O'Flynn writes that as users 'choose one video clip from one community' they also 'subordinate the other community', deciding to whom to give 'voice and agency' and who, conversely, to render silent (O'Flynn, 2015, 80). I think the term 'complicity compulsion' is helpful in explaining this. In *Gaza Sderot*, and in aspects of many other i-docs, engaging with the i-doc requires users to be implicitly complicit with a situation they may prefer to contest.

The German word 'zugzwang' describes a situation found in chess and other 'turn-based' games. It translates roughly as 'compulsion to move'. This is where a user has to move but has no good choices; any move made (within the rules of the game) will make their position worse not better. Complicity compulsion is a sort of equivalent in i-docs. Users have to do something if they want to progress the experience, but the choices available to them sometimes don't include moves they (ethically) want to make.

The i-doc *How to Create a Financial Crisis* does something similar. To progress the narrative users are required to submit answers to questions, but they are not given options to contest how financial systems work (and lead to crisis), only to agree. For example, one statement about how regulations are used to the advantage of people in positions of power is followed only by the option to press 'Happens everywhere!' Other statements about corruption and injustice are followed only by options to press 'Ok ...'. By giving the user nominal interactivity, but only offering prescribed answers, this i-doc creates complicity compulsion and demonstrates how difficult it is not to comply with global financial systems.

So, bearing in mind that both interactivity and its absence are important to be intentional about in i-doc design, here are some questions you can ask yourself when thinking about interactivity in your i-doc:

Box 5.1: Ideation notes for interactivity

- How obvious should interactive capacities be? Should some be more obvious than others?
- How often should users have to interact to progress the action?
- What kinds of interaction do you want to include? Questions? Choices of what to see next? Games/challenges? Comment options? Options to submit users' own content?
- What kinds of calls to action do you want to make? How explicit should these be?
- When a user interacts how open should their choices be? Should there be a range of options, or just a nominal click-through to accept a continuation of events?
- Should there be any responses to user interaction? For example, if users answer a question do they get feedback? Or do meters or tallies change depending on what they do?
- Should there be events or demands that interrupt users during other content? If so, what, when, and how often?
- How obvious should limits to interactivity be? Which limits should be more obvious than others? Are there any you particularly want to foreground?
- Should all users experience the same interactive capacities and frustrations or is this dependent on how they interact?

Answering these questions by thinking firstly about what your answer will be and secondly about *why* that's the right answer will illuminate your research topic and in particular, I think, help you consider issues of freedom and compliance related to it.

I-docs and digital freedom

Before moving on to talk about *The Lockdown Game* I'm going to briefly talk about two i-docs that use the design of their interactive features to focus on freedom and complicity in digital space. As a digital medium and method, i-docs are well placed to help researchers to explore and understand digital spaces and lives.

Universe Within is an i-doc I've already mentioned. It's part of the series 'Highrise'. To explore *Universe Within* you have to pick one of three narrators who introduce themselves as 'digital natives'. These narrators boast about the fluidity and freedom that their digital constitution allows them. One explains that she can retrieve data about the 'real' world by instantaneously moving between places in a way that 'makes aeroplanes seem kind of old school'. Users have to be taken everywhere by these narrators and, in return for being transported, must answer survey-style questions. This frustration of agency (making movement contingent on giving information) highlights the fact that digital explorations may feel seamless but actually involve giving large amounts of information to companies and organisations who monitor and monetise that data. Accessing the i-doc requires the user to comply with this process. The implicit other option is to find this information without the help of digital avatars, using the 'old-school' systems of physical exploration alluded to.

A similar technique is used by the i-doc *Digital Me*. This i-doc works by mining the user's data (the user gives it access to their email and social media) in order to produce a narrative personalised to them. In order to access this promised personal story, users have to comply with the data-gathering process. Again, this i-doc uses interactivity to shed light on how, in navigating digital space, we are complicit in the monetisation of our own data. However, unlike *Universe Within*, *Digital Me* enlists user agency at the beginning, to access the data, and then writes the story for you. When I used the i-doc I found the story produced for me frustrating as the assumptions made from my data weren't accurate (it thought my PhD supervisor was my romantic partner, presumably because she was my most contacted person in the period it examined!). The frustrations of agency here, then, illuminate how little power we have over what's done with our own data after we give platforms access to it. While the promise is of a personalised story, what comes back (at least for me) exposes the lack of real attention to individuals in the way these processes work. I hope these two interesting i-doc projects can inspire the use of i-docs as methods to explore digital worlds and their politics.

Freedom and compliance in *The Lockdown Game*

One of the most remarkable findings of the research that took place through *The Lockdown Game* was how notably participants' views on freedom and compliance changed during the process. Of course, the changes in their views likely arose, in part, from living through lockdown itself, but I think it's clear from an analysis of the participatory i-doc-making process that i-doc design was key to how their new opinions formed too.

At our second i-doc-making workshop, the interactivity group was put in charge of all decisions about interactive capacities and limits. The discussion members had focused on how they could use frustrations of agency to echo the frustrations they experienced during lockdown and, relatedly, how they could highlight the difficulty of decision making with regards to whether or not to comply with lockdown rules.

This group used a Miro board (shared digital ideation platform) to take notes during their breakout group. On this Miro board they added notes about how the well-being and viral-risk meters could work. They also had sections of the Miro board titled 'frustrating interactions' 'new rules coming in', and 'restrict access to i-doc'.

Many ideas that didn't end up being included in the final i-doc design (mostly because they were very technically complex to implement!) are interesting in what they reveal about how the group encountered lockdown via i-doc making. For example, one idea they had was that i-doc visitors would have to join a virtual queue to access some content and would have to 'social distance' by restricting the number of people who could access the i-doc at any one time. These features were designed to express the day-to-day experiences that made lockdown feel frustrating and stifling. Equally interesting were the group's ideas for what they called 'frustrating the interaction'. These include many features that did make it into the final i-doc, such as the pop-up windows offering injections of bleach or invitations to buy loo roll as well as one which wasn't fully realised but did have some follow-through: that 'some things don't have the effect you expect'. This idea materialised in having the viral-risk and well-being meters change in unpredictable ways sometimes. The group had more dramatic ideas, but we decided it would be too disorientating for audiences to have radically unexpected things happen as these may feel like errors rather than part of the experience.

The group also imagined that there could be rules given to the user that turn out to be contradictory. For example:

> You can go to someone's window to visit them but someone's already there – but you can go and wait in the pub, but then your risk of getting Corona has just gone up ... or you can only bulk buy [toilet roll] in 100 but then they're sold out.

Other abandoned suggestions for agency frustration included a discussion about cutting off the audio or the visuals for periods of time during the user's experience to signify periods of shielding or isolation during lockdowns, when contact and mobility was even more limited than normal.

Through their discussion of these ideas the group arrived at an analysis of how their freedom felt violated during lockdown. This wasn't because of the restrictions in and of themselves. The majority of the group were happy with the principle of having restrictions in place to stop the spread of the virus. It was because the group felt that the restrictions were pretty much futile in actually stopping the virus because they were so badly thought through and contradictory. Because of this, the rules seemed designed more to frustrate people than to do any actual good.

This satire of lockdown rules continued in the group's design of the i-doc's ending. After much debate it was decided that the i-doc *should* have an ending point but participants couldn't agree about what this ending should constitute. Eventually, they decided to have multiple optional endings that users can choose themselves. The optional endings, which appear after ten minutes, read as follows:

> Wow it feels like this lockdown has been forever! Want to escape? ...
> a. Make an illegal trip to your countryside property!?
> b. Take your chances with herd immunity!?
> c. Boost your vitamin C and hope for the best?
> d. Suck it up and wait for the vaccine?
> e. Have some fun then come back for lockdown 2?
> f. Embrace your newfound social anxiety and stay in lockdown?

These options playfully reflect the range of hopes and behaviours at the forefront of public consciousness during the pandemic. They include options to violate rules in order to escape, including by making an 'illegal trip to your countryside property', but the subtext is that this is only available to the wealthy (who would have such countryside properties). The other options involve either staying in lockdown or chancing infection. Again, the design of these optional endings develops a critique of freedom during lockdown, here emphasising how freedoms were unevenly distributed.

The optional endings of *The Lockdown Game* are a false promise though. Whichever ending the user chooses they'll soon find that all options actually take them back to the start of the i-doc. This was a second level of satire designed by the group. The second i-doc-making workshop (where the majority of the design work happened) took place during a second lockdown period in the UK in November 2020. This lockdown saw the introduction of another new set of rules, more complex than those of the first lockdown (this time they introduced a tier system that dictated which areas were on what level of lockdown, along with a set of convoluted rules about travelling between tiers). By this point participants (and most of the rest of the country) were exasperated by the prospect of continued restrictions with no clear end in sight. They were frustrated that the government had put in place policies like 'eat out to help out' over the summer (a policy that provided discounts on meals to encourage people back into restaurants), only to then put everyone back in lockdown following the predictable rise in cases of the virus. The deceptive ending to the i-doc reflects the groups' exhaustion at trying to comply with yet another iteration of complex and nonsensical lockdown rules.

In *The Lockdown Game* then, the audience experiences an intense compliance compulsion. It comes in the form of being required to make choices to balance well-being and viral risk even though the choices made don't actually make a difference, meaning users are compelled to play an unwinnable game. This is most emphatic in the i-doc's ending, where the user must make a choice but none of the options on offer will actually take them out of lockdown.

An existential experience

The agency frustrations and compliance compulsions that the group designed demonstrate their sense of the absurdity of how the pandemic was managed in the UK. In their discussions, participants explored the idea of expressing this by imposing rules in the i-doc that changed continuously, reflecting their feeling that the real rules were being made up on the fly without logic behind them. One participant, Beth, had the idea that the i-doc should start 'very formal and rules based at the beginning' but descend into a situation where 'anything goes ... make your own rules up cause everyone else is!' She elaborated:

> [How about] for the first 2 minutes everything is risky but the next 4 isn't ... so one person might think something's completely safe but the next person who looks at the same thing – it's more risky ...

She explained that this was essentially how real lockdown rules had felt:

> [D]on't wear a mask, do wear a mask, things are okay, things aren't okay, we're in lockdown, we're not, go to a pub ... always ever changing rules ... you can do the same things two days in a row and it be a risk or no risk.

The bombardment of pop-up windows in the i-doc was intended to reflect this experience of ever-changing instructions. As the audience navigates the i-doc, they'll gradually realise that the rules and suggestions being thrown at them don't make sense and have no essential relationship to what actually happens to them as they explore its content.

The lack of logical rules or consequential actions means that the user's navigation in the i-doc is somewhat aimless. There is no way of winning or completing the i-doc. There is no reward for keeping your viral risk low, no consequence for keeping it high, no implications for how well you balance your well-being, and the options at the end throw you back into lockdown regardless of what you choose. *The Lockdown Game* is game-*like* but there is no prescription about what it means to succeed in that game or what users should get from it. In linear media, we can sit back and be told a story, confident that it's going somewhere, that it has a purpose. In many i-docs, and certainly in *The Lockdown Game*, we don't get to do this; we have to construct a meaning for ourselves.

This decision to have no externally prescribed way of winning the lockdown game, but to require the user to make their own meaning based on what they encounter, echoes an experience of lockdown as a vacuum of life's normal prescribed meanings. With so many of the externally prescribed tasks we're normally subsumed into stripped away, people found themselves needing, much more than normal, to decide for themselves how they wanted to be in the world. Like lockdown itself, the i-doc is a space for wandering and wondering, detached from the normal expectations and projects that we treat as essential. The expanse of non-prescribed time and empty spaces that many of us experienced in lockdown is evoked by a lot of the content the group made: photos of empty streets and parks, uncanny views of the deserted city of London, and footage of seemingly mundane activities like cooking or cutting hair that felt newly strange and fascinating. The user wanders through the i-doc's pages and contents with the same combination of lack of purpose and sense of renewed fascination that many of us experienced during the pandemic. As they explore the i-doc's contents, they construct their own meaningful experience; a meaning that isn't externally prescribed but is derived from their own engagement.

I'd argue that this analysis of life during lockdown via the i-doc is akin to an Existential realisation. The group didn't put it in those terms, but what they identified could easily be framed in Existentialist language. Framed in that language, this would be the realisation that we are 'condemned to be free' (Sartre, 1946, 5), that there is no essential meaning to life, just the meanings we create. Lockdown certainly prompted this experience for many. Waking up on the first day of lockdown and finding that all the rules, norms, and routines we lived by had been changed overnight allowed us to see the contingency of those rules and thereby glimpse the essential truth that (in the words of the late David Graeber) 'the world is something that we make and could just as easily make differently' (Graeber, 2015, 89).

At follow-up interviews that I conducted after the i-doc was finalised many participants told me that the discussions we had while making the i-doc had made them more critical about their compliance with rules in general.

Aga, for example, eloquently explained:

> [Lockdown] changed my relation with the world: I have to rely on myself, find my own solutions ... I see the world now ... the world is more divided between followers and people who make their own decisions ... those who just want to stick to the rules even though they're not making any sense.

Although she respected 'that other people don't have the same attitude', she was, 'at the same time', 'more and more assured that certain rules are very, very stupid' and 'those who make the rules are not very clever'.

Co-producing the i-doc's critique of lockdown rules had strengthened Aga's resolve that not only these specific rules were nonsensical but that most prescriptions about how to live should be treated with scepticism.

Beth, likewise, noticed herself becoming more likely to take decisions based on her own reasoning rather than on rules or expectations. When I asked her if making the i-doc had changed her own relationship to rules (as it had for Aga) she started by saying that she was the kind of person who doesn't question rules and expectations, and that that hadn't really changed. But then, pausing to contemplate it properly, she changed her mind:

> I probably dismiss quite a lot of rules now … thinking about it. … If there's a one-way system, I might think, I'm just going to walk this way … I think I have actually [become less compliant], thinking about it – definitely, actually, yeah.

For Nuria, this new critical perspective was even more pronounced. She described 'a profound change in whether I trust the government and trust the state'. Nuria told me that before she 'just accepted that things work in favour of the public most of the time … but now I'm wondering if a lot of the systems we uphold actually don't … are not optimal … don't benefit people the way we should'. She determined that 'I probably feel more defiant now … I'm not just going to comply with rules or laws just before they exist or because we're told it's wrong not to comply … I have more respect for any kind of rebellion … even if I hold completely different views … people were doing very human things [that] became rebellious during this time.'

Clearly then, participants had a shared experience of becoming more critical of rules and compliance with them. Freedom had come to mean something new to them, something existential. As I said earlier, I'm sure this change in perception came largely from living through a pandemic. But I also think that making *The Lockdown Game* developed and refined their critique of rules and compliance, and certainly allowed them to articulate that critique collectively.

Designing interactive components of i-docs means designing rules for somebody else to live by, albeit for a short period of time. The interactive capacities that you include, and those that you deny your audience, dictate what people can and can't do within your i-doc. Designing interactive components of an i-doc is, then, essentially designing a system of governance. But at the same time, as explored previously, your design will invite a particular mode of spectatorship that might include an invitation to be sceptical or critical. *The Lockdown Game* definitely invites audiences to be sceptical of its own, and any other, systems of governance.

I-docs have vast potential for enabling attention to freedom, rules, and compliance, as well as to agency, as has been much discussed already by i-doc theorists. From my participants' experiences of making *The Lockdown Game* we can see how clearly i-doc making can bring questions of freedom and compliance into focus. Encountering the world through i-docs heightens our critical awareness of the construction of rules and expectations as well as our experiences of freedom and its limitations.

6

Co-creation and multi-perspectivity

> **Key chapter arguments**
>
> - I-doc methods can help participants to define shared worlds without effacing differences.
> - I-doc methods can counter epistemic injustice by allowing publics to co-create knowledge.

Co-creation and multi-perspectivity

So far the chapters of this book have focused on particular components of i-doc making – temporal architectures, spatial infrastructures, aesthetics, and interactivity. I've discussed the modes of encounter that designing each of these components catalyses and shown the values of those forms of attention for research. In this chapter I switch the focus to processes of i-doc making and, in particular, to co-creative processes.

I-docs lend themselves to co-creative making. Because they showcase multiple discrete pieces of media content within an interface, they are often used for projects that seek to include multiple perspectives. There's been a huge amount written about co-creative methods as well as about co-creative processes of digital media production and I won't repeat all that here. Instead I'm going to talk about three key values of participatory i-doc making.

Table 6.1: Key terms

Key terms	
Collective thinking tool 'Thinking tools' is a commonly used term to describe frameworks, prompts, and physical and digital activities that enable different kinds of thinking	Any tool (digital or analogue) that enables people to think together. I argue that i-docs are great collective thinking tools.
Imagined community (Anderson, 1983)	From Benedict Anderson, a community that we feel we belong to even if we might not know or ever meet some of the people in it (eg a nation or supporters of a football team).
Shared spaces for difference My invention	A space (conceptual or physical) that is inclusive and collective but accommodates difference. I argue that i-doc-making processes can offer these spaces.

Firstly, I'll explore how using i-docs as a participatory method can create shared worlds without homogenising differences. I'll do this with reference to the participatory process of making *The Lockdown Game*. I'll discuss how, despite their diverse identities, conflicting political opinions, and varying choices of how far to comply with lockdown, my participants came together at the workshops to create a shared vision for the i-doc and, in doing so, created a collective analysis of what lockdown should teach us about the world and ourselves. As such, I suggest that i-docs can be crucial tools for catalysing thinking about how to build consensus without minimising or denying division. I'll also use this case study to discuss how researchers can use participatory i-doc making to investigate how participants make sense of and negotiate diverse and divergent experiences and perspectives. It's been argued that story-based methods can get participants 'dialogically involved', inviting them to 'think about their [own] thinking and not only be objects of my thinking' (Paulo Freire in Nuñez-Janes et al, 2017, 30). Participatory i-doc making definitely enables this. It requires participants to discuss their own experiences, ideas, and processes together and, with you as a researcher, engage in this second-order thinking.

Secondly, I'll examine the values of co-creative i-doc making within activist projects. I discuss *Athens Report* and *18 Days in Egypt*, which both collect user-contributed footage to document political situations (the Egyptian uprising of 2011 and the Greek debt crisis). These i-docs provide a platform where anyone can upload materials. I'll talk about how these kind of projects can counter 'epistemic injustice' and draw out how this capacity can be highly valuable for social researchers who are working with activist methods and methods for change (Kara, 2017; Pickerill et al, 2021; Pottinger, 2021).

Then, thirdly, I'm going to talk about how i-doc-based methods can tell stories with multiple heroes. Within my role on the AHRC programme StoryArcs I've been leading the creation of a series of interactive, multimedia digital resources that will allow 'story associates' (postdoctoral researchers partnered with host organisations) to contribute their ideas and research findings to what we're calling an 'i-story': an interactive output showcasing the meanings and values of story skills.

The Lockdown Game: shared worlds for difference

I've already described the process of making *The Lockdown Game* so if you're not reading sequentially I recommend having a look at Chapter 3 where I detail the different stages of the design process. There are also extensive discussions in most of the other chapters on the participatory process of *The Lockdown Game*'s making, including how participants worked together at online workshops and in breakout groups to make design decisions. Here I won't go back over the practicalities of the process extensively but instead will focus on what emerged from that process: how the i-doc making experience enabled collective thinking while also holding on to different opinions and perspectives.

My participants were a diverse group of people from two areas of London, Deptford and Dalston. I'd recruited them from these areas because, as I mentioned earlier, the initial plan for the project was to make a participatory i-doc about how class distinctions are articulated, reproduced, and transformed in gentrifying areas. Once lockdown was imposed this became impossible, so the i-doc ended up being about lockdown itself.

Further than being from those two gentrifying areas of London I didn't have any particular recruitment criteria, but I was aiming to enlist participants from a broad class spectrum (because of the original project remit). I used flyers in shops, gyms, barbers, and so on, in each area, as well as digital flyers on local Facebook group pages, to recruit. I held introductory conversations with everyone who expressed interest. These initial one-to-one conversations were important for building rapport and connection with each member of the group. I made clear that contact hours within the project (time in workshops and interviews) were paid at £20p/h. This payment was important to: (a) make sure that finances weren't a barrier to taking part; and (b) honour participants for their contribution to knowledge.

The group I ended up working with reflected a range of different ages, class positionalities, nationalities, and political standpoints, and included people with disabilities and neuro-divergences. A failure in my recruitment was that no Black participants were included in the final group (although two of my participants had Black partners and dual-heritage children whose experiences feature in the i-doc), despite both areas of London having large Black Caribbean and Black African populations. This may reflect my positionality as a White researcher and lack of detailed knowledge at the time of how to engage diverse participants. I think it also reflects the disproportionate stresses of lockdown itself, as three Black participants who had initially signed up dropped out of the group when lockdown was imposed. They didn't give me a reason but, given what we know about how COVID-19 placed unequal pressures and risks on minority ethnic groups, it's reasonable to infer that they had bigger things to think about at that point than taking part in a research study. Indeed, the impact of COVID-19 and lockdown precluded many participants from taking part. One White woman in her 20s who had initially signed up had to drop out because of the amount of work involved in applying for relief when her business was forced to shut.

I also had a lack of participants of retirement age. One woman in her 80s, who had initially been keen, dropped out when lockdown forced the activities to take place online. She didn't feel computer literate enough to take part independently and although we made plans for a neighbour to help her it became too complex in light of social-distancing rules. The other skew in participants was that they were predominantly female (11 out of 13). Although the group I originally recruited had a more proportionate gender spread, it was predominantly women who agreed to stay with the project after the pandemic hit, although I'm not sure why. One interesting finding from the recruitment process was that the project seemed to appeal to recent mothers. As you can see from the clips in the i-doc, I had several women take part who had had babies very recently (and one who had her baby during the research period). I suspect the project appealed to these women as a way to do something creative and structured with relatively low time requirements while on maternity leave.

In some ways, then, lockdown was a very difficult time to undertake participatory research. On the one hand, the pressures of the pandemic led to several initial sign-ups dropping out and, even for those who stayed, many were struggling during the pandemic with financial pressures, worry about elderly relatives, shielding because of health issues, homeschooling children, and so on. On the other hand, the participants who stayed in the project were a captive audience! Once lockdown started, due to their particular circumstances, they had much more time and focus on the project than they would have done otherwise and this is probably reflected in the quantity and quality of the material they produced for the i-doc (one woman going as far as to document everything she ate and everywhere she walked over a period of several weeks).

Broadly speaking, my remaining participants were people who were less (relatively speaking) precarious during the lockdown period and therefore had time to give to the project. That said, they did include one person awaiting visa decisions to see if they could stay in the UK, another with multiple health issues and disabilities who was shielding, another doing frontline work in the NHS, another who was pregnant during the pandemic, and several people experiencing housing insecurity; that is, living in places inappropriate to their needs and/or having to move during the pandemic.

Interestingly for the project, my participants also reflected a fairly broad political spectrum. Because they were recruited from

Deptford and Dalston (gentrifying areas of London) they were, on balance, definitely politically left leaning, but they had very different responses to the imposition of lockdown, underscored by different perspectives and assumptions about governance. For example, one woman, Holly, made a film for the i-doc that clearly voices her resistance to lockdown, as well as her resistance to the internal rules of the housing co-op she was living in at the time. Her film documents how, upon hearing that lockdown was being imposed, the immediate response of her and her friends was to have a party, in explicit defiance of the rules. Holly's frustration, as voiced in the film, is in part at how other people took it upon themselves to police lockdown rules as dictated by the government, rather than making their own assessment about what was safe and reasonable. For example, she documents neighbours within the housing co-op who are 'snitching' and threatening to call the police 'because we [apparently] need to isolate every house even though we share a communal garden'. In her film, Holly and her friend compare the situation to being in a prison where certain prisoners have self-selected to be complicit with the guards in policing the other prisoners. Holly's position is as much to do with her political principles (which I'd read as being broadly in line with anarchism) as it is to do with scepticism about the virus itself. At one point in the film she explains that 'I get the science, and I get the maths, but I can't not fight the politics.'

Meanwhile, other people in the group were much more compliant with lockdown rules and quick to adopt government advice around hand washing, social distancing, and mask wearing, once it came into effect. As I've discussed in previous chapters, the process of making the i-doc caused many of the group to become more critical of lockdown rules and rules in general – but their views were still on a wide spectrum and this is reflected in their content, which often shows how far, and in what ways, they felt the need to break or bend rules. While Holly's film shows full disregard for the rules, other pieces of content show compliance, for example in pictures and clips of visiting friends and neighbours at their windows and keeping to social-distancing rules. In other submissions we can see people inventing their own ways to keep contact with loved ones while honouring the spirit of lockdown. For example, one very surreal video shows Sylvia's mum greeting

Co-creation and multi-perspectivity

her grandson while wrapped in sheets of see-through plastic and wearing goggles. Content submitted by participants also shows a spectrum of political, social, and cultural affiliations, from Aga's content about joining London Renters Union and being active in anti-eviction protests, to Megan's content about joining her parents in celebrating VE (Victory in Europe) day.

One of the key values of i-doc making as a participatory method is that i-docs can put different experiences and narratives not just into proximity with each other but into relation. *The Lockdown Game* showcases a variety of heterogeneous pieces of content, diverse in style, medium, and in the experiences and perspectives expressed. These pieces of content were made by participants in their own time, based on loose instructions that I put together with my artistic lead Jack Scott, which included suggestions about the type of things they might capture, the mediums they might use, and the amount of material that would be appropriate to submit. Participants created the material before meeting each other at the first workshop. Each of them had an online meeting with Jack to discuss any edits they wanted made before the content was assimilated into the i-doc. For example, some participants wanted Jack's help editing photos and videos, adding voiceovers, captions, and so on.

Because the heterogeneous content that participants created can be viewed separately and in any order, it is able to speak for itself without being subsumed into a narrative that makes a particular argument. Yet, at the same time, such content sits within the co-designed i-doc interface and is therefore part of a shared world. Indeed, the group were emphatic about their desire to make the i-doc a shared world. After a discussion at the workshops, they decided that content should be tagged to show who made it but should be organised thematically – linked to objects – rather than organised by person (eg the interface could have been a list of people, where you clicked on their name to see their experiences). They also, as I discussed in Chapter 4, decided that the images used as backdrops in each area of the i-doc, and the soundscapes for indoor and outdoor regions, be made by collaging together bits from all of their content. If storytelling can be a 'bridge between people at a critical time of class, racial and ethnic division' (Nuñez-Janes et al, 2017, 15) then i-doc making, as a form of storytelling, constructs this bridge while also expressing the differences between the positions it connects.

The participants made active choices that produced an i-doc which emphasised connection over division. They had free rein (within time and budget constraints) over its design so could have, in theory, decided to categorise content by how compliant people were with the rules, by where people lived, or by other differentiated aspects of their experience – such as whether they had children, were shielding, were furloughed, and so on. The fact that, from this open starting point, they designed the i-doc interface as a house and local area that was literally an amalgamation of their content makes clear that they felt they had had, to a large degree at least, a shared experience.

The format and duration of the i-doc-making workshops I held also enabled this collective approach. I made sure that there was time built in for people to properly introduce themselves, ask each other questions, and discuss the materials they'd produced with the rest of the group. I also used a quite informal facilitation style, setting the tone for friendly and explorative conversations. It was important that participants built strong relationships with Jack and Michael Skelly too as they were co-facilitating elements of the workshops and, more importantly, were in charge of realising the participants' vision. Michael's account of his experience of making *The Lockdown Game* (in Box 6.1) shows how important it was for him to connect with the participants and fully understand their vision.

Box 6.1: Michael Skelly, technical lead

Working on this i-doc was a technical project like no other. Usually, software projects have a simple goal – we want some software that achieves certain functionality and does so in the most efficient way possible. And, mostly, the UX of a digital experience is crafted with one aim in mind: allowing the user to access and interact with the information as easily as possible. There is a single, although sometimes hard-to-quantify, measure of success: Did people manage to do the thing they were trying to do as efficiently as possible?

There are also a large number of patterns and best practices for how to achieve this.

In this project however, accessing the information as efficiently as possible wasn't exactly the aim. Unlike a standard documentary, where the themes and meaning are expressed solely through the content, we believed that for an i-doc, the experience of consuming the content – the UX – should also communicate the themes and meaning of the overall work.

So we really had to throw away all the usual rules and best practices of UX, which were optimised for displaying content in the most efficient, understandable way possible, and come up with entirely new paradigms, where the experience of consumption mirrored and enhanced the overall message.

That gave us three big challenges when creating this interactive work: creating something whose form helped communicate the themes; making sure that it still ended up as a piece of content that was engaging to consume; and realising the work using the technologies available.

For the first, we turned away from standard UX frameworks and looked to a different field.

In the theory of video-game design, games are analysed by looking at mechanics, behaviours, and aesthetics. Mechanics are the explicit rules of the game, as coded by the programmer. For example, in a horror game, there might be a mechanic that says 'the player can't both hold a torch and wield a gun at the same time'. Behaviours are the changes in how a player acts in response to the mechanics. So, the mechanic of the torch/gun choice might lead to behaviour where the player needs to move quickly in dark areas and constantly scan for threats. Then the aesthetics are the feelings and emotions elicited in the player from the behaviours the mechanics have caused: the player feels vulnerable and scared while moving through dark areas.

In producing this i-doc, we tried to communicate and enhance the theme and meaning of the content by producing aesthetics that mirrored the feeling and emotions experienced by the participants during the time in lockdown and expressed through their content – feelings of being trapped, of frustration, of unexpected moments of joy, and many more.

Some of this we managed to do through mechanics that were also thematically relevant to the experience of lockdown. We tried to engender a feeling of disbelief and frustration by adding 'pop-ups' that introduced arbitrary rules, mirroring the arbitrary rules imposed during lockdown. Others we did with mechanics that were entirely artificial (for example, on-screen meters that allowed the users to quantify their mood and energy levels) and not part of the lockdown experience (nobody could actually quantify those things!), but that still produced thematically relevant behaviours (having to balance a mix of different activities to fill the time) and ultimately gave the aesthetics we wanted (the user feeling like they had many things they could do, but not sure which one would give them what they needed).

At the same time, however, we needed to make sure that the content was still accessible and that the experience wasn't frustrating; or at least not introduce accidental frustration that was entirely unrelated to the themes of the work! Although our documentary would be interacted with in a novel and thematic way, users needed to at least be able to understand what they were seeing and how to interact with it, in order to be able to understand the thematic and aesthetic impact.

For this we adopted user-interface paradigms that would be familiar to most users, although not usually associated with consuming a documentary. Many of the elements were adapted from video games, such as 'health-bar'-style meters to represent mood and energy, or a 'point-and-click' interface to explore a virtual house.

We also explored mechanics that encouraged behaviours that lead to the consumption of the actual content: ensuring each piece of content had a different impact on the mood and energy of the character encouraged the viewer to explore different options, and having pop-ups that forced the user 'to go outside' allowed us to ensure that they visited areas that might otherwise have been missed.

Finally, we needed to actually realise the work, by building it in code. Throughout the process, we had to balance the ideas that we all had for showcasing the content in thematically relevant and experientially compelling ways with the reality of creating this with a fixed deadline and budget.

This was an iterative process, often done in real time, of having the participants express what they were looking to achieve and me trying to work out what would be possible within the limits of the technology we were working with, and then pitching back something that I felt captured the spirit of what they wanted (eg the mechanics, behaviours, and aesthetics) but still fit within our technological limitations. So, a 3D house you could explore with a first-person virtual camera turned into a 2D house in fixed perspective, but which could nevertheless still be explored room by room.

The iteration also continued after we'd locked down the conceptual ideas: it wasn't until we actually implemented the mechanics that we got to experience the emergent behaviours that we had theorised might come from them and feel the aesthetics that did – or didn't – arise. And so, from the original concept, we added and removed mechanics (added a hover effect to indicate what's interactive), tweaked the parameters (how often should the pop-ups show?), and tuned the overall experience to the actual content we were putting in (how much energy should this video clip grant the character?).

Ultimately, in order to address the three challenges, the final product was a mix of tradeoffs: Which of the possible themes would the mechanics prioritise? How much should we prioritise the aesthetics of the i-doc versus making its content readily accessible? Which of our ideas should we cut in order to be able to make this technically possible? Making those tradeoffs in a sensible way was only possible through building this as a dialogue between documentary maker, participants, and technical creator.

However, no matter what the participants had chosen, the design would have been a joint endeavour. It might not have reflected the camaraderie I think *The Lockdown Game* does, but by definition it would have had to reflect some kind of consensus – even if that consensus was an agreement to disagree. This is because the task of the participants wasn't to submit content to be subsumed into a platform that I would design but to design the platform itself.

This meant that, as well as creating their own individual pieces of content they had to work together to produce something shared: a digital creation that reflected shared convictions and decisions about what lockdown was like and how it should be communicated to audiences. Even had they decided to create an i-doc that divided content into discrete segments – for example, grouping content by levels of compliance or deciding that each person's content should be on a different page – that would still have been a decision arrived at collectively. This is why I think i-doc making as a participatory method is so impactful. It requires participants to work together to build something shared, at the same time as it allows different individual perspectives to be portrayed.

The group I collaborated with to make *The Lockdown Game* generally worked together happily and seamlessly. Although there were definitely more dominant and quieter group members, and the odd moment of tension around political or cultural differences, there was no hostility and no disagreements that couldn't be amicably talked through. Having not run the same project with other groups, I obviously can't draw conclusive statements as to what underscored this positive co-creation culture. However, one of my assumptions is that disagreements or serious tensions that might have arisen among this group of people in other circumstances were mitigated because they weren't discussing lockdown itself but, instead, how it should be represented in their i-doc. I'm pretty sure that if I'd asked the same group to design a social-distancing policy, or if I'd asked them simply to discuss their views on the pandemic, many fairly serious disagreements would have arisen. Focusing on the i-doc, though, took the heat out of the conversation.

As we've seen in previous chapters, the group arrived at a shared critique of lockdown rules via making the i-doc. Despite differences in levels of compliance and scepticism, they created something that reflected a shared experience of finding the rules absurd and frustrating. Where they couldn't reach a consensus, the non-linear format of the i-doc allowed multiple perspectives to be included without having to choose one overarching narrative.

From my perspective as a researcher, it was valuable to be able to watch participants debating and discussing how to design the i-doc. The conversations they had enabled me to see in which areas there was consensus and where there were sticking points, and to observe how they negotiated the design around these. I'd advocate for this as a great method for researchers who want to understand convergent and divergent experiences and ideas within a group of people, or who want to study how people can reach common ground despite different starting points. While taking the heat out of direct debates about socio-economic, cultural, or political issues, i-doc making creates a space where a group negotiates differences and alignments.

Audiences and imagined communities

There was another, more unexpected, way in which the participatory process of making *The Lockdown Game* created a sense of a shared world. The group designed elements within the i-doc that connected their experiences to that of wider society, including the imagined community of the i-doc's audience.

The creation of this imaginary of a wider community comes in two forms in the i-doc. Firstly, there are requests that pop up as you're playing, asking you questions like 'Did you speak to your parents today?' or 'Did you check in with your friend?' The group discussed how these prompts should represent the need to care for others as part of what 'winning' lockdown requires. Sylvia suggested that you might 'get extra points if you call a friend who's feeling lonely'. However, the group also considered that it could be made unclear to the user what caring for others looks like within the lockdown game. Beth had the idea that, when watching a video about a member of the group, the user could be asked whether they want to continue watching it but, crucially, not be told that the request to continue 'represents checking in'. This would mean that you might choose not to continue, without realising that leaving the video early indicates a lack of care for the person the video is about. This reflected the struggle people had experienced with knowing how to care for others during lockdown, when the normal ways we show care – visits, hugs, spending time together – were restricted.

Secondly, reminders of the well-being of the collective were integrated into the i-doc by links to external sites that the group wanted to attach to some of the content. These sites include news stories, Facebook pages for mutual aid groups, community activism pages, and so on. As I mentioned previously, this suggestion was made by group members who were worried that the satirical tone of the i-doc might be read as undermining the gravity of the virus and its impacts. The majority of the workshop had focused on the ridiculousness of the rules and the humour in that, but as the process drew to a close several members of the group became concerned that the magnitude and very real tragedies of the pandemic needed to come across in the i-doc too. The links were included so that audiences who had had difficult experiences could be signposted via the i-doc to support groups or helpful resources. Observing the design of these elements made me realise that the group had enacted another kind of shared world building by making the i-doc. By imagining their audience, they had developed concern for a wider collective and designed ways to support them.

Imagined communities is a term coined by Benedict Anderson (1983) to describe communities that people feel part of even though they might not actually interact with most of the people encompassed in them. For example, a nation is an imagined community. In making *The Lockdown Game* I observed how participatory i-doc projects can make both temporary communities (a group of people who come together and find a shared vision within a time-bound project) and imagined communities (an idea of a wider collective who might invest in and benefit from engaging with the i-doc).

Through my work on crisis cultures[1] I've explored how contemporary life is defined by intersecting crises. I've seen how crises can lead people into more and more siloed ways of thinking, including by prompting conspiratorial thinking, losing trust, and doubling down on class distinctions. I think i-docs can be a mode of encountering the world that holds on to multi-perspectivity while also enabling us to find common ground. In this vein, Judith Aston has argued that i-docs can offer the kinds of narrative we need for this polarised world. As she's explored, whereas conventional models of story focus around a singular

---

[1] See the website www.crisiscultures.co.uk for more info on this.

hero defeating adversaries, i-docs can tell stories with multiple heroes and emphasise collaboration not conflict (Aston, 2022).

In an era defined by multiple compounding crises, widening political divides, and a 'post-truth' culture, we need ways of gathering and telling stories about the world that enhance understanding of intersection and connection, marry polyvocality with critical investigation, and enable compassion and collaboration between diverse groups. I think i-doc making enables these crucial modes of attention.

Activist i-docs and epistemic justice

In the next part of this chapter I'm going to talk about co-creative i-docs with an explicitly activist inflection. I-docs are often made as part of social, political, or environmental justice movements and campaigns. Many of these are co-creative – seeking to bring the perspectives of 'ordinary people' to the foreground rather than just that of a film director. I want to talk here about two quite similar i-doc projects, *Athens Report* and *18 Days in Egypt*. Focusing, respectively, on the Greek debt crisis and the Egyptian uprising of 2011, both of these collate user-contributed footage to document alternative accounts of contentious political situations. Made in pivotal political times, these i-docs seek to counter what Miranda Fricker has defined as 'epistemic injustice' by providing a platform where anyone can upload materials and contribute to how history is narrativised. I-docs of this kind serve as a 'carrier bag' (Le Guin, 2019) for collecting experiences, rather than as a mode of storytelling premised on opposition and conflict (as Ursula Le Guin describes beautifully in her essay *The Carrier Bag Theory of Fiction*).

Epistemic justice refers to the injustice done when marginalised groups are disregarded as knowers (excluded from knowledge production) and/or deprived of the concepts they need to make sense of their worlds (because accessible and rigorous knowledge is predominantly produced by elite groups – who have the resources to do so – and therefore serves their purposes rather than the needs of the marginalised). For example, researchers have explored how women are not taken seriously when giving accounts of sexuality and sexual violence (Cuthbert, 2022; Messina, 2022), young voices are excluded from key climate justice decisions (Murphy, 2021), Black voices are excluded within social movements (Ferreira, 2022), and the digital 'public sphere' is disproportionally produced by White, Western European, and North American men, meaning that information online predominantly serves their needs (Acey et al, 2021). Fricker explains these as 'testimonial injustices', which occur 'when a prejudice causes a hearer to give a deflated level of credibility to a speaker's world', and 'hermeneutical injustices', 'when a gap in collective interpretive resources puts someone at an unfair disadvantage when it comes to making sense of their social experiences' (Fricker, 2007, 1).

These epistemic injustices not only silence marginalised people, they also hold us, as a global society, back from making sense of the complexities of multiple, compounding crises facing us. If only the dominant voices are heard and amplified, then we will never fully understand the world and its challenges. Within work on epistemic injustice, there is a call for methodological approaches that can produce knowledge in more epistemically just ways (Marovah & Mkwananzi, 2020; Walker et al, 2020; Mkwananzi & Cin, 2021). I would argue that i-docs can be a great way of achieving this, offering a method that can facilitate more egalitarian means of producing and sharing knowledge.

In *Collective Wisdom*, Cizek and Uricchio argue that co-creative media can tackle the 'epistemological fragmentation' of the contemporary era (2022, 295). I'd add to this that co-creative methods, and i-docs in particular, can also tackle epistemic injustice. In fact, I'd argue that tackling epistemic injustice is a necessary step before tackling epistemological fragmentation. We can't meaningfully bridge divides in what people hold to be true, and in what they think constitutes knowledge, until there is more equality in who produces knowledge and who is taken seriously as a knower.

However, equalising the epistemic playing field is becoming more and more challenging. The rise of phrases like 'post truth' and 'fake news' make clear how much distrust there is of information in public discourse, as well as how easy it is to discredit information. Historians Robert N. Proctor and Londa Schiebinger have used the term 'agnotology' (2008) to refer to the deliberative cultivation of ignorance. There are many forms of agnotology, from the production of 'deep fakes' that show politicians supposedly saying things they never said, to the casual spread of misinformation on social media, as people retweet and repost claims without any sense of their veracity.

It's also very complicated to work out what should count as acceptable knowledge. It would be easy to paint the issue as a battle between sanctioned expertise and media mis/disinformation. But, as Fricker's work emphasises, what counts as sanctioned expertise is decided by gatekeepers in academia, government, and government-adjacent institutions that are themselves embedded in a history of colonial, sexist, racist, heteronormative, transphobic, and ableist oppression. Within these trusted institutions there are long histories of deliberate exclusion of minoritised voices. In short, they enact their own versions of misinformation by deliberately prioritising the agendas of a small, privileged group. This issue is compounded by the dominance of colonial languages on the internet, with huge inequalities existing online regarding which languages information is written and available in. It's also being further compounded by the growth of AI technologies, which work by pulling together existing online material in order to produce new content. By definition this reproduces and amplifies existing inequalities in what exists, and doesn't exist, online.

This context makes it more important than ever to bring underrepresented perspectives to the foreground. I-docs like *18 Days in Egypt* and *Athens Report* try to do this. *18 Days in Egypt* is an i-doc launched by Jigar Mehta on 25 January 2012: the one-year anniversary of the Egyptian revolution. As Mehta describes, the launch was not of 'our final product' but 'the beginning of our documentary about the revolution. Our audience is our collaborator.'

18 Days in Egypt is a platform where the audience are encouraged to submit their own documentations of the Egyptian uprising. It launched with content that was created by beta users over a two-week period. Six young Egyptian journalists and students were hired as 'field producers' to help people to upload content and gather stories from those without internet access. People were encouraged to contribute 'their footage, their photos, their e-mails, their texts, even their Tweets and Facebook status updates, all created during the last year in Egypt, particularly, but not limited to the first 18 days of the uprising, January 25 to February 11, 2011' (Mehta, 2012).

This co-creative process was especially politically poignant given that during the Egyptian uprising the government had tried to quell protests by cutting off social media access. There were also efforts to destroy accounts of the government's misconduct by storming the offices of charities and non-governmental organisations (NGOs) who documented human rights abuses and, in the months and years following the uprising, to stifle revolutionary narratives by imprisoning journalists. In this context, *18 Days in Egypt* is radical in providing a platform via which people can tell stories from their own experience, producing a collective counternarrative in the face of attempts to control the story. The simple interface of *18 Days in Egypt* presents each contribution in an equally sized square, visually indicating the equality of all narratives and keeping the authorial voice minimal.

Athens Report also works by crowdsourcing contributions, this time to document protests in Athens during the Greek debt crisis of 2008. This i-doc has more authorial curation than *18 Days in Egypt*. Compared to the plain design of *18 Days*, which foregrounds content, *Athens Report* has a more elaborate interface, embedding content onto a map of the route of a number 11 trolley bus, which 'travels across the city center connecting neighborhoods with significant role to the sociopolitical history and the urbanisation of Athens'.[2] *Athens Report* also contextualises user submissions by including a 'dates and links' column that has a timeline of relevant events and information.

But, like *18 Days*, the content is 'continuously uploaded by individuals and collective who were actively engaged in the public space from 2008 to 2015 producing their own narratives on the experience of Athens as a city in "crisis", a subject of global media attention and a battleground'. The authors state that the map design is intended to 'leave space for countless interpretations to emerge'. Again, then, this i-doc seeks to use user-contributed content to create counternarratives in a contentious political climate. The makers describe it as 'a common ground, built through the visitor's experience of urban space and protest'.[3]

---

[2] https://athensreport.org/
[3] https://athensreport.org/

Clearly these projects still have some degree of authorial control. However, certainly compared to traditional documentaries, they shift control away from the people with cameras and technological resources (who are likely to be those already in more epistemically powerful positions) and potentially enable perspectives to be foregrounded that normally wouldn't get airtime. To fully activate their potential as an epistemically just method, I'd argue that participatory i-doc making should be used as part of 'scholar activism', where researchers 'spend time in a place, observing and experiencing what happens in the daily lives of individuals in that setting' and building trust and understanding (Pickerill, 2021, 2). This would mean that authorial and curatorial decisions made by the researcher about the processes and products of i-doc making can be more in line with the needs and desires of the people the i-doc concerns. It will also mean that activist scholars do not just advocate for communities (Hale, 2006) but can facilitate knowledge production by that community. As Hale's edited collection notes, the efforts of activist scholars to progress political causes can clash with demands for 'rigour' and 'objectivity' in academic research. These institutional cultures and policies are precisely the kind of mechanisms that reproduce epistemic injustice though, and only make more pertinent the kinds of knowledge production that co-creative i-docs enable.

I think there is exciting potential here for researchers looking to counter epistemic injustice. I-docs can create an infrastructure within which research participants and wider publics can create knowledge themselves. The multimedia formats of i-docs also mean that participants can use whatever medium they find most accommodating, as is invited by *18 Days in Egypt*. Activist i-docs like these two projects foreground multiple perspectives but they also insist on the multi-perspectivity of all and any stories. The ongoing invitations on both these platforms for audiences to upload their own content emphasises that these are not, and can never be, complete stories, because all perspectives will add something. These platforms both show the potential of i-docs as a method not just for academic research but for research for change led by charities, NGOs, advocacy groups, activist groups, community groups, and so on. The collective behind the

Methods for Change project highlight that 'Given the complex and interconnected problems the world is currently facing, this is an important moment to mobilise the potential of social science methodologies with non-academic stakeholders' (Barron et al, 2021). I agree and think that co-creative i-docs, like the ones discussed in this section, can be a fantastic way to create the epistemically just knowledge that we need to drive epistemically just changes.

A story with multiple heroes

I-docs and related forms can also be used to tell stories with multiple heroes. As mentioned previously, scholars, including Judith Aston, have argued that the contemporary world needs stories that emphasise collectivity not conflict (Aston, 2022). At a time of intensifying political and social polarisation, it's crucial to find models of storytelling that allow us to connect, collaborate, and comprehend the experiences of others.

This is a model we're progressing in the AHRC-funded programme StoryArcs, led by Professor Bambo Soyinka at Bath Spa University. The aim of StoryArcs is to explore and define a 'Story Skill Set' that will help people to understand and articulate story skills and their applications. StoryArcs operates at both programme and placement level. We have a central research team as well as associate researchers (Story Associates) who undertake placement projects with a range of host organisations (UK-based businesses, charities, and other institutions). The Story Associates receive training and mentorship, while addressing challenges set by their host organisations using their story skills.

My role in StoryArcs is to lead on knowledge exchange between the Story Associates and the internal StoryArcs research team so that the Story Skill Set can be co-produced. In order to facilitate this two-way exchange, I'm creating a series of interactive, digital packs. The packs are a two-way interface: they share content and materials from our internal research with the Story Associates, while also providing ways for the Story Associates to share ideas and findings from their projects with us.

As the programme progresses, we'll be taking forward the material shared through the packs to create an 'i-story'; an interactive documentary of sorts that will showcase the multiple and intersecting ways that the Story Associates' projects illustrate the Story Skill Set. The i-story will tell a story with multiple heroes. Each project is its own adventure but by bringing them into dialogue we can pinpoint, analyse, and communicate commonalities in how story skills are developed and deployed. As we've seen across this book, this is a strength of all i-docs. The i-doc is a medium that lends itself to bringing multiple narratives into a shared space – illuminating and generating intersections without conflating differences.

I hope this chapter has given some indications of the co-creative potentials of i-docs as methods. I've argued that researchers can use participatory i-doc making to do work that finds common ground without erasing differences, and to study how groups of diverse people negotiate differences to arrive at shared conclusions. I've also shown how i-docs can be used to counter epistemic injustice as well as how they can tell stories with multiple heroes.

Of course, a barrier to using i-docs within activist projects and as methods for change can be that the costs and technological requirements prohibit researchers with small budgets and communities of participants with low access to media technologies. In Chapter 7 I'm going to explore how these barriers can be overcome by making i-docs with low-tech, easy-to-use tools or by *thinking* with i-docs without the need for any digital platform at all.

7

Thinking with i-docs

Key chapter arguments

- There are many user-friendly platforms that enable low-tech and low-budget experiments with i-doc making.

- You can also 'think with i-docs' without needing to create anything digital, by using the template I provide for a generative thought experiment.

- I-docs are an important method for the contemporary moment, because the modes of encounter they develop are useful for exploring, articulating, and responding to intersecting crises and compounded precarities.

In the chapters of this book so far, we've explored the modes of encounter that i-doc making offers. As I argued in Chapter 1, making an i-doc engages and develops ways of seeing, thinking, imagining, and sensing that are distinctive to i-docs as a cultural form. As I've shown, the distinctive modes of encounter that i-docs offer are incredibly fruitful and constructive in relation to research and can add nuance and precision to our analysis of topics. I've shown how temporal architectures can help us think about time and its politics, how spatial infrastructures can draw our attention to distributions of power, how aesthetics can focus our attention on the interplay of affects at different scales, how interactivity can attune us to complexities of freedom and compliance, and how co-creative i-doc making can be a way to find common ground while also holding onto difference. Needless to say, I'm a big advocate for the power of i-docs as method.

However, there are many barriers to making an i-doc as part of a research project. They require a significant budget and/or technical skills in filming, editing, and coding. Another challenge is that, as web-based media, it's very easy for i-docs to stop working if the website isn't maintained or if the platforms they are built on become outdated or discontinued. A significant number of early i-docs no longer work because a version of Flash they were built on became defunct and, presumably, the makers didn't have scope or budget to recreate their work using new tools.

In this book I'm interested in the value of the i-doc-making process as much as in the final product, but obviously it's still preferable if the final product has some longevity! To give your i-doc the best chance of surviving long term online I'd recommend:

- Doing thorough research and seeking professional advice on the best platforms and software to use at the time of making. If you're working with a web developer, they should be able to advise on this.
- Hold a budget back for potential updates. Things are changing so fast in the digital world at the moment that it's likely that, at some stage, your platform will need minor or major work to update it to run on new technologies. If at all possible, try and keep some of your budget back for updates you might need down the line.
- Selecting a platform that's 'too big to fail'. For example, in some of my less complex i-doc projects I use the platforms Genially and Canva. On the one hand, Genially is a relatively small and unknown platform so I know it's feasible that, one day, my Genially creations won't be accessible anymore. Canva, on the other hand, is a burgeoning creative tool used by many industry professionals as well as amateur creatives so I expect that they will have a plan for ensuring people's creations survive any updates to their mechanisms.

- Document your i-doc. If your i-doc *does* end up going offline you'll want to have thorough documentation of what it was like when it was live. Make sure you have screenshots, screen recordings, and backups of all of the content in your i-doc.

The tips given should help to mitigate issues with keeping i-docs alive online. However, budget and expertise are still going to be barriers to i-doc making. To make i-docs accessible as a method it's therefore key to extract the cognitive tools they offer so that they can be used in low-tech, low-budget settings and so that they don't depend on particular technologies.

I'm keen to show how the modes of encounter developed through i-doc making can be extracted from the actual process of creating a digital interface. This way, the value of i-docs as a method can be more widely taken up and used by researchers without the technical competencies or resources needed to build an i-doc. In this chapter I give a practical template for how you can 'think' with i-docs that can be used by readers in their own research. The questions I've suggested in previous chapters are used to form the template, becoming part of a comprehensive thought experiment for considering how you would hypothetically make an i-doc about your topic. This way of planning i-docs is developed from a workshop I ran as part of the Methods Lab at Goldsmiths University, where I asked researchers to design (using only A3 paper and felt tips) an i-doc about their topic, an exercise they found highly valuable. It's also been inspired by collaborative work with Judith Aston where we've explored the value of i-docs as a thinking tool for crisis times and argued for the importance of extracting cognitive tools from i-docs (Harris & Aston, 2022). The template I provide for i-doc planning focuses on the component elements of the process that the book has discussed. I argue that what is key for social research isn't learning how to replicate commercial i-doc projects. Rather, it is to understand the conceptual tools that i-docs as a new media have generated and progressed, and then to harness these in whatever ways are most conducive to understanding and improving the world.

This chapter will also signpost readers towards some free/low-cost (depending on the version) platforms that I've experimented with using to create i-docs and other interactive digital thinking tools: Canva and Genially. These platforms are both very user-friendly and give significant flexibility in designing an interactive, digital, multimedia site without needing any expertise in coding or even much confidence with technology. There are also platforms designed specifically for making non-linear films, such as Klint and Korsakov, which Anne Marie McIntyre has given a great account of in an essay.[1] Personally, I prefer working on Canva and Genially as they give much more flexibility in interface design, are easier to create your own aesthetics in, and are geared towards a mix of media rather than just film; all of which I think are important if the cognitive capacities of i-doc platforms are to be fully harnessed within a design process. I think these platforms are good options for researchers who want to use i-doc-like methods in a low-budget, low-risk way, where they still have a large amount of creative control.

As I mentioned in Chapter 1, part of the reason that I'm so keen to promote i-docs as a method *now* is because I think the modes of encounter that they develop are incredibly useful in the contemporary moment, which is defined by intersecting crises and compounded precarities. In this context I think it's an important time to make those modes of encounter more widely deployable. My own research is mostly about how precarity and crisis manifest in and are made sense of through cultural phenomenon and cultural discourses. My excitement about i-docs comes partly from how useful I've found i-docs to be in thinking through precarity and crisis. I've made these arguments elsewhere. For example, in a blog I wrote in 2016 for the i-docs research group website (i-docs.org) I argued that the spatial and temporal logics of i-docs (as non-linear forms) closely relate to the logics of the contemporary condition and can therefore be used to make sense of it. This relationship is not a coincidence. As I examined in Chapter 1, media emerge from and respond to the logics of the eras they are developed within. As I explained in the 2016 blog, the non-linear spatio-temporality of i-docs gives them a particular purchase on precarity that can make them a

---

[1] https://ammaci.wordpress.com/essays/korsakow-and-klynt-a-brief-analysis/

great method for exploring and expressing 'the spatiotemporal conditions currently undergirding and ensuing from precarity' (Harris, 2016).

In another blog for i-docs.org in 2022, co-authored with Judith Aston, we argued that i-docs are also particularly valuable for understanding crises. We built on findings from the co-organised symposium 'I-Docs, Crisis and Multi-Perspectival Thinking' to argue that the 'polyvocal capacities, nonlinear logics and multimodal properties [of i-docs] make them a good fit for interrogating and communicating crises as complex, precarious situations where diverse perspectives cannot be conflated into one narrative, and ways of moving forward are multiple'.[2] Here, the emphasis is on how i-docs can bring multiple stories into proximity with each other without positioning them adversarially. In this blog we discussed how this aptitude of i-docs makes it important to extract the 'language' of i-docs as a tool for thought.

Thinking with i-docs: a template

Table 7.1 provides a framework for encountering your research subject through i-docs. You can also access a digital version by following the link.[3] I'd like to invite readers to use this template to plan an i-doc about a research topic you're currently working on or have worked on, and to see how the process enhances your thinking. The template compiles the questions from each chapter, prompting you to think about the different components of i-doc making – designing temporal architecture, spatial infrastructure, aesthetics, and interactivity. It also includes questions about what kind of i-doc-making *process* would be relevant for your project (the who, what, where, when, and why of i-doc making), including decisions about if you should employ the co-creative capacities I discussed in Chapter 6.

The primary purpose of this template is for you to use in a thought experiment. The aim is that by planning a hypothetical i-doc, you'll learn something new (or hopefully many things!)

---

[2] http://i-docs.org/thinking-with-i-docs-cognitive-tools-for-uncertain-times/

[3] https://www.progresstoday.co.uk/thinking-with-i-docs-template

Table 7.1: Thinking with i-docs: prompts

Thinking with i-docs: prompts	
Processes (who, where, when, why?)	Who: Will you design this alone? Are you a team? Will this involve participants or publics? Where: Does this design occur within a research 'field' or as part of a workshop? What space or environment is needed/appropriate for this design process? And what tools? When: Does this design happen in one sitting? Is it an iterative process? Does it follow or respond to an event? How: What is your process? Will sections of the design be allocated to particular groups or people? Are decisions to be made through reflection or through further research?
Temporal architecture	• Should there be an order in which your audience is made and/or encouraged to look at pieces of content, or should it be up to them? • Should there be pieces of content that can *only* be accessed after other content? • Should all pieces of content be visible to the audience at once, or should they be on different pages or in different sections so that audiences are encouraged to watch groups of clips together? • Should there be pieces of content that can only be accessed once, or for a limited amount of time, or should your audience always be able to come back to them? • Should there be an introductory page or sequence to the i-doc and if so how long should your audience be required or encouraged to spend on it? • Should the user have a limited amount of time in the i-doc? Does it 'finish' at a particular point or can they explore it indefinitely? If it does finish, how? • Should there be any limitations on the amount of the i-doc's content that the user can view in one sitting? Are there things you don't want to give them time to watch or do completely? • Should there be any restrictions on when the i-doc can be accessed?
Spatial infrastructure	• Should all your content be visible at once on the same page, or do you want your user to have to discover content? • If the latter, what should the pathways to discovery be? Is the user required to scroll down, up, or through content (either moving to the right or to the left), or do they click between different pages to see groupings of content? Or, are there a combination of different 'discovery pathways'? • Should content be visible immediately or revealed by clicking on an icon or object? If the latter, what should these icons or objects be? • Should the layout of your interface be stable, or do you want pieces of content to move around depending on what the user does?

Table 7.1: Thinking with i-docs: prompts (continued)

	Thinking with i-docs: prompts
	• Do you want to use a map, diagram, chart, list, or some kind of other structuring device to show relationships between and/or groupings of pieces of content? • What other kinds of screen-based media do you want your interface to be most similar to? A game? A database, article, timeline, video game, map? • Do you want more than one option for how users encounter content? For example a map view and a database view, or a page that structures content along a timeline and then another page that groups it thematically?

Aesthetics	• What is the mood/feel that's appropriate to create for this i-doc? Should it be playful? Scary? Dramatic? Surreal? To create this mood/these moods, what are the appropriate choices of:
	  o fonts
	  o colour schemes
	  o icons
	  o soundscape(s)
	  o sound effects
	  o styles of arrows and other orientation devices.
	• How much movement should there be on the screen to create the right feel in your i-doc (including how surreal or lucid you want it to be)? Do you want a static image as the backdrop, a video clip, or a backdrop with subtle movement?
	• What mode of spectatorship do you want your audience to approach the i-doc with? As an experiment? As a creative work? As a journalistic piece? As a direct encounter with your participants? What kind of aesthetic choices will signal this? What are the appropriate choices in relation to:
	  o amount of explanatory text
	  o signposting/nudging for how to use the i-doc
	  o information about the project.
	Reconsider all the things in the list so far (fonts, colour scheme, soundscape, sound effects, arrows, and orientation devices) with these elements in mind.
	• Think about whether there should be variations in different aspects and elements of your i-doc – should pieces of content have different moods/feels/atmospheres to the interface? Should there be different pages or segments with different atmospheres? Should there be a shift at a temporal point where the mood/atmosphere changes? And so on.

Interactivity	• How obvious should interactive capacities be? Should some be more obvious than others? • How often should users have to interact to progress the action?

(continued)

Table 7.1: Thinking with i-docs: prompts (continued)

Thinking with i-docs: prompts
• What kinds of interaction do you want to include? Questions? Choices of what to see next? Games/challenges? Comment options? Options to submit users' own content? • What kinds of call to action do you want to make? How explicit should these be? • When a user interacts how open should their choices be? Should there be a range of options, or just a nominal click-through to accept a continuation of events? • Should there be any responses to user interaction? For example, if they answer a question do they get feedback? Or do meters or tallies change depending on what they do? • Should there be events or demands that interrupt them during other content? If so, what, when, and how often? • How obvious should limits to interactivity be? Which limits should be more obvious than others? Are there any you particularly want to foreground? • Should all users experience the same interactive capacities and frustrations or is this dependent on how they interact?

about your research topic. Sandra Gaudenzi has also developed a template for planning an interactive digital storytelling platform (the !F Lab Field Guide) but her template presupposes that you're making something digital. Of course, you can use my template to make a digital i-doc too, but it doesn't work on the premise that you will.

To use this template, first decide what topic you want to encounter via i-docs. I'd recommend that this is a topic you've already researched because the prompts will require you to think about nuanced details of that topic. That said, I've had workshop participants tell me that the exercise was really generative in thinking through plans for research they were about to embark on.

Once you've chosen your topic, decide if you want to use this template on your own to enrich your personal thinking about a topic, if you want to use it with a research team to develop your collective thinking, or if you want to use it with research participants to learn about how people whose worlds you're studying understand a topic. You could also use it in a teaching setting to help students to articulate their understanding of a research subject with more precision. Then, go through the table and, for each area of i-doc making, think about what would be the most appropriate process/design strategy for your research topic and, crucially, *why*. The *why* is what will really enrich your thinking, by prompting you to think carefully about the logics of your topic in order to imagine how those logics could be expressed in an i-doc.

If you're using the template in a group, you might want to think collectively but you could also start by creating designs individually and then compare and debate them. Debating differences between your own design and that of another member of your research team will help you to identify nuanced convictions about your topic and work out if you are in complete agreement or have different perspectives.

This template is something you might use to think with more than once for the same research topic. It might also prompt new or deeper investigations if you realise that you don't have answers to some of the questions about i-doc design and need to know more about your subject to be able to answer these. If you're thinking with i-docs as part of a participatory project, then the process might help to identify areas of convergence and divergence in people's experiences or perspectives that can help to shape directions for future work.

Working with lower tech platforms

If you want to go beyond i-docs as a thought experiment and make an interactive digital site, but don't want (or have the means) to undertake a complex coding endeavour then this section introduces some platforms you can use. The two platforms I discuss, Canva and Genially, are the ones I've used in my own lower tech experiments with making interactive digital resources. They're both very user-friendly and don't require prior experience. You can pick up the basics pretty quickly with a day or so of experimenting. Canva is very widely used, mostly for graphic design purposes. Genially is less well known. There are many other platforms that could be used to make i-docs; I'm focusing on Canva and Genially simply because they're the ones I know, but I'd encourage you to do your own investigating, especially as new platforms and apps are being released and updated all the time. (For example, I've recently started experimenting with a platform called Visme too.)

Neither Canva nor Genially are explicitly designed for making i-docs, but, coming to them with a knowledge of i-docs, I quickly saw how they could be used in that way. Genially was actually designed to make interactive learning resources and is mostly used by educators, but you can make anything interactive on it. Canva, as I said, is mostly used for graphic design purposes, but again it's very flexible. Both platforms allow you to publish your creations to a web link or embed them in an existing site. Often, I've used Canva and Genially together, either making aesthetic elements on Canva (which is better for design) and uploading them into Genially (which is better for interactivity) or making an interactive element on Genially and embedding it into a Canva design (or doing both, as you can embed elements from one into the other and then back again)!

One of the first things I made on Canva was a piece called *Epistemic Fragmentation* that was published in a collage journal called *ctrl v* (Harris, 2023). I call this an interactive collage rather than interactive documentary because it doesn't contain documentary content per se, but it's also a way of doing and communicating research in an interactive and non-linear fashion. This piece isn't based on primary research but on secondary research I conducted into the idea that our ways of knowing and conceptions of what knowledge is are becoming increasingly divergent in a polarised society. Because this is one of the first things I ever made on Canva there are a lot of features and tricks I didn't include that I would now. Canva has also been updated since and now has new capacities, a lot of which use AI to make once incredibly complex design manoeuvres very simple.

In *Epistemic Fragmentation* I designed a series of pages within Canva's 'presentation' template that could then be published either as a scrolling document or a presentation-style click-through site. The pages are designed with collages made from graphics, images, and videos available within Canva's internal library as well as other content I uploaded (usually this was images or videos I downloaded from other websites but I also included some content I filmed/photographed myself). I positioned these items on the pages to create collages, layering, adjusting, and adding elements until I was happy with the aesthetic. The collage style reflects the idea of fragmentation. For the most part, the images and graphics I've used relate to themes that splintered out of the content I was reading or engaging with during this research. For example, one article I read was about emojis as a form of language, which is why there are emojis decorating that page. There are also a lot of graphics of plants included in the designs. These are a reference to a scene in the TV series 'The Good Place' where Janet (an all-knowing eternal being who can conjure up any information or object that a person/being asks for) loses her skills in a system reset and starts presenting people with house plants when they make requests, rather than with what they actually asked for. This scene was interesting to me in how it communicated the breakdown of a connection between information that comes in and information that comes out, so I used plants in the aesthetic design to connote a similar disconnect in contemporary political discourse. Once I'd made my collages, I embedded links to articles, books, podcasts, and so on that I'd been consuming on the topic, which is very easy to do in Canva, via a button that associates a web link with any text or object. I tagged the links onto coloured dots and added animated graphics of pointing fingers as clear pathways of discovery.

I also embedded question forms into the pages using an integrated app called Typeform. This is easy to do using the 'app' function in Canva, which links the platform with multiple other platforms and apps. The question forms elicit responses from the audience. Some questions are more about prompting reflection on the theme than actually gathering information (eg the 'Do you speak this language' and 'Is your brain on multiple sides of the epistemic fracture' questions are intended to make the user to think about their own position and experiences. But I also included questions that asked users if they wanted to share anything where they could leave more substantial answers. I used the free version of Typeform so was only able to collate a certain amount of responses, but it was great to see the responses I did get (which I won't quote as I don't have the writers' permission) and to know that the piece prompted other people's reflections and learning. I was also able to see how often different pages had been viewed in this way, which can be very helpful when you're trying to measure the impact of your research.

Where Canva lacks is in designing the temporal architecture of interactive digital platforms. There are ways of guiding or prompting users to access content in a particular order, but it's hard to be that prescriptive in Canva (eg by interrupting them with questions, kicking them out of pages, making some content only available once other content has been explored or certain activities completed). For that reason I also work with Genially, which is less flexible for aesthetic design (it has a less extensive library of aesthetic components and is less user-friendly and flexible in how you can manipulate images and visuals) but is great for interactivity. It's very easy to embed questions for your users as well as videos, sound, text, and images into pages. It's also easy to create interactive buttons that link to pop-up boxes or other pages, or that play audio or show text when you hover over them. You can also make objects draggable very easily.

A group of French teachers, operating under the name 'S'cape' have also created their own code snippets that you can copy and paste into your designs to enable more complex interactivity. Ones I've used as lot include a function that turns an object, image, or shape into something a user can write in (so their text is visible on the screen); functions that make objects appear, disappear, or get larger when you bring another object near to them (eg you can make a magnifying glass magnify a small object or a lamp illuminate something hidden); functions that make objects move around when the user clicks; functions that make something appear or happen at a certain time or after a user clicks in all the right (or wrong) places; and many others. These features are being updated continuously. They're a bit more complex to use because you have to follow instructions that aren't always straightforward to understand (and are sometimes in French!) but they still require no ability to code or understand code and there are helpful YouTube videos and presentations explaining how to use them (in English)!

I've yet to make a full i-doc in Genially, but I've used the program to make many i-doc-like resources. These include educational resources for work I do in schools and pupil referral units, ideation activities to use at research focus groups, and thinking tools for research programmes and research departments of organisations. These aren't i-docs, but are other great examples of how interactive digital resources can benefit educators and researchers as thinking and learning tools. I've also used Genially to make experimental i-doc-like creations such as *Boxing Life*, an interactive collage I made about retiring from elite-level boxing. I hope that exploring these low-tech i-docs and interactive resources that I've made will give you ideas about how you can use these platforms to incorporate i-docs as a method into your own research.

I strongly believe that the modes of encounter i-docs produce are incredibly valuable in making sense of the world around us, providing 'perceptual equipment' (Jameson, 1991, 80) equal to the complex and multiple issues that define our present day. As researchers, our task is to develop modes and mechanisms of investigation that can illuminate and intervene in important topics. In putting energy into developing i-docs as a method, my aim is to generate modes of encounter that enable me, my collaborators, my participants, and other research teams to better understand our world and how to improve it. I'd love to know if this book has been helpful to you in catalysing and developing your own thinking. Please feel free to contact me and share your experiences of thinking with i-docs!

APPENDIX

Interactive documentaries referenced

18 Days in Egypt: https://www.18daysinegypt.com/
A Journal of Insomnia: https://docubase.mit.edu/project/a-journal-of-insomnia/
Athens Report: https://athensreport.org/theproject/
Boxing Life: https://view.genially.com/64e12ae92002b800184fc6de
Corona Haikus: https://coronahaikus.com/
Digital Me: http://i-docs.org/digital-me-is-more-than-your-digital-you/
Epistemic Fragmentation: https://www.ctrlvjournal.com/issue13/harris.html
Gaza Sderot: https://gaza-sderot.arte.tv/
Going North: https://goinnorth.org/
Hollow: http://hollowdocumentary.com/
How to Create a Financial Crisis: https://www.nfb.ca/interactive/how_to_create_a_financial_crisis/
I Can Almost See the Lights of Home: https://www.albany.edu/jmmh/vol2no1/lights.html
Journey to the End of Coal: https://docubase.mit.edu/project/journey-to-the-end-of-coal/
Migrant Mothers of Syria: http://www.morningbirdpictures.com/migrant-mothers-of-syria.html
One Shared House: https://onesharedhouse.com/thestory/
Quipu Project: https://interactive.quipu-project.com/#/en/quipu/intro
Refugee Republic: https://refugeerepublic.submarinechannel.com/

Roo Tongue: https://root-tongue.com/community-gallery/
Seven Deadly Digital Sins: https://sins.nfb.ca/
Stories of Change: https://www.open.edu/openlearn/nature-environment/creative-climate/stories-change-duplicate2?page=1
Terminal 3: https://1ric.com/terminal-3
The Chicago 00 Project: https://chicago00.org/
The Lockdown Game: https://lockdown-idoc.netlify.app/
The Temporary City: http://thetemporarycity.com/ (password TTC)
The Universe Within: https://docubase.mit.edu/project/highrise-universe-within/
The Waiting Room: https://victoriaapplebeck.com/immersive/the-waiting-room-vr/
Witness 360: 7/7: https://eastcityfilms.com/witness-360

References

Acey, Camille, Siko Bouterse, Sucheta Ghoshal, Amanda Menking, Anasuya Sengupta, and Adele Vrana. 2021. 'Decolonizing the internet by decolonizing ourselves: challenging epistemic injustice through feminist practice'. *Communication and Media*.

Ahmed, Sara. 2014. 'Not in the mood'. *New Formations*.

Alexandra, Darcy. 2017. 'More than words: co-creative visual ethnography'. In *Deep Stories*, by Mariela Nunez Jane, Aaron Thornburg, and Angela Booker. De Gruyter.

Allen, John. 2011. 'Powerful assemblages?' *Area* 154–7.

Anderson, Benedict. 1983. *Imagined Communities, Reflections on the Origin and Spread of Nationalism*. Verso.

Anderson, Ben. 2009. 'Affective atmospheres'. *Emotion, Space and Society* 77–81.

Anderson, Ben. 2014. *Encountering Affect: Capacities, Apparatuses, Conditions*. Routledge.

Anderson, Ben, and Colin McFarlane. 2011. 'Assemblage and geography'. *Area* 124–7.

Ash, James. 2009. 'Emerging spatialities of the screen: video games and the reconfiguration of spatial awareness'. *Environment and Planning A*.

Ash, James. 2015. *The Interface Envelope: Gaming, Technology, Power*. Bloomsbury.

Aston, Judith. 2022. 'Interactive documentary: re-setting the field'. *Interactive Film and Media Journal* 7–18.

Aston, Judith, Sandra Gaudenzi, and Mandy Rose. 2017. *I-Docs: The Evolving Practices of Interactive Documentary*. Wallflower Press.

Back, Les, and Nirmal Puwar. 2012. 'A manifesto for live methods: provocations and capacities'. *The Sociological Review*.

Barron, Amy, Alison Browne, Ulrike Ehgartner, Sarah Hall, Laura Pottinger, and Jonny Ritson. 2021. *Methods for Change*. Manchester University.

Bastian, Michelle, Lisa Baraister, Michael Flexer, Andrew Hom, and Laura Salisbury. 2020. 'Introduction: the social life of time'. *Time & Society* 289–96.

Bauman, Zygmunt. 2000. *Liquid Modernity*. Polity.

Belanger, Daniele, and Rachel Silvey. 2020. 'An im/mobility turn: power geometries of care and migration'. *Gender, Security & Human Rights* 3423–40.

Bennett, Jane. 2005. 'The agency of assemblages and the North American blackout'. *Public Culture* 445–66.

Bennett, Jane. 2010. *Vibrant Matter: A Political Ecology of Things*. Duke University Press.

Benzon, Nadia von, Mark Holton, Catherine Wilkinson, and Samantha Wilkinson. 2021. *Creative Methods for Human Geographers*. SAGE.

Berland, Lauren. 2011. *Cruel Optimism*. Duke University Press.

Bissell, David. 2021. 'A changing sense of place: geography and COVID-19'. *Geographical Research* 150–9.

Bonilla, Yarimar, and Jonathan Rosa. 2015. '#Ferguson: digital protest, hashtag ethnography, and the racial politics of social media in the United States'. *American Ethnologist* 4–17.

Bowman, Benjamin, and Sarah Pickard. 2021. 'Peace, protest and precarity: making conceptual sense of young people's non-violent dissent in a period of intersecting crises'. *Applied Youth Studies* 493–510.

Boyd, Douglas, and Mary Larson. 2014. *Oral History and Digital Humanities: Voice, Access, and Engagement*. Palgrave.

Butler, Toby. 2006. 'A walk of art: the potential of the sound walk as practice in cultural geography'. *Social and Cultural Geography* 889–908.

Campt, Tina. 2023. *A Black Gaze: Artists Changing How We See*. MIT Press.

Chan, Nadine. 2020. 'Pandemic temporalities: distal futurity in the digital capitalocene'. *Journal of Environmental Media*.

Chang, Anita Wen-Shin. 2020. *Third Digital Documentary: A Theory and Practice of Transmedia Arts Activism, Critical Design and Ethics*. Peter Lang.

References

Churcher, Millicent, Sandra Calkins, Jandra Bottger, and Jan Slaby. 2023. *Affect, Power, and Institutions*. Routledge.

Cizek, Katerina, and William Uricchio. 2022. *Collective Wisdom: Co-creating Media for Equity and Justice*. MIT Press.

Coleman, Rebecca. 2010. 'Dieting temporalities: interaction, agency and the measure of online weight watching'. *Time and Society* 265–85.

Coleman, Rebecca. 2020a. 'Making, managing and experiencing "the now": digital media and the compression and pacing of "real-time"'. *New Media and Society* 1680–98.

Coleman, Rebecca. 2020b. 'Refresh: on the temporalities of digital media "re"s'. *Media Theory*.

Coleman, Rebecca, and Jessica Ringrose. 2013. *Deleuze and Research Methodologies*. Edinburgh University Press.

Cosgrove, Denis. 2008. *Geography and Vision*. I.B. Tauris.

Crary, Jonathan. 1990. *Techniques of the Observer on Vision and Modernity in the Nineteenth Century*. MIT Press.

Crary, Jonathan. 2002. 'Géricault, the panorama, and sites of reality in the early nineteenth century'. *Grey Room* 5–25.

Cresswell, Tim, and Craig Martin. 2012. 'On turbulence: entanglements of disorder and order on a Devon beach'. *Tijdschrift voor Economische en Sociale Geografie* 516–29.

Cuthbert, Karen. 2022. 'Asexuality and epistemic injustice: a gendered perspective'. *Journal of Gender Studies*.

Davies, William. 2018. *Nervous States: How Feeling Took Over the World*. Jonathan Cape.

DeLanda, Manuel. 2013. *Intensive Science and Virtual Philosophy*. Bloomsbury Publishing.

Deleuze, Gilles, and Felix Guattari. 1987. *A Thousand Plateaus: Capitalism and Schizophrenia*. University of Minnesota Press.

DeSilvey, Caitlin. 2007. 'Art and archive: memory-work on a Montana homestead'. *Journal of Historical Geography* 878–900.

DeSilvey, Caitlin. 2012. *Anticipatory History*. Uniformbooks.

Deuze, Mark. 2011. 'Media life'. *Media, Culture & Society* 137–48.

Deuze, Mark. 2023. *Life in Media: A Global Introduction to Media Studies*. MIT Press.

Dijn, Annelien De. 2020. *Freedom: An Unruly History*. Harvard University Press.

Dittmer, Jason. 2010. 'Comic book visualities: a methodological manifesto on geography, montage and narration'. *Transactions of the Institute of British Geographers.*

Doel, Marcus, and Clarke David. 2007. 'Afterimages'. *Environment and Planning D: Society and Space.*

Fahim, Joseph. 2021. 'How the Arab Spring changed cinema.' BBC. https://www.bbc.com/culture/article/20210113-how-the-arab-spring-changed-cinema.

Fahim, Joseph. 2023. 'Palestinian ghost stories: how filmmakers are using the supernatural to confront the wounds of the Nakbu'. Middle East Eye. https://www.middleeasteye.net/discover/palestine-nakba-filmmakers-ghost-stories-confront-wounds.

Favero, Paolo. 2013. 'Getting our hands dirty (again): interactive documentaries and the meaning of images in the digital age'. *Journal of Material Culture.*

Favero, Paolo. 2017. 'In defence of the "thin": reflections on the intersections between interactive documentaries and ethnography'. In *Refiguring Techniques in Digital Visual Research*, by Edgar Gomez Cruz, Shanti Sumartojo, and Sarah Pink. Palgrave.

Ferreira, Priscilla. 2022. 'Racial capitalism and epistemic injustice: blindspots in the theory and practice of solidarity economy in Brazil'. *Geoforum* 229–37.

Forket, Kirsten. 2017. *Austerity as Public Mood.* Rowman & Littlefield.

Fricker, Miranda. 2007. *Epistemic Justice: Power and the Ethnics of Knowing.* Oxford University Press.

Gallagher, Michael. 2020. 'Voice audio methods'. *Qualitative Research* 449–64.

Garrett, Bradley. 2011. 'Videographic geographies: using digital video for geographic research'. *Progress in Human Geography.*

Garrett, Bradley, and Harriet Hawkins. 2014. 'Creative video ethnographies: video methodologies of urban exploration'. In *Video Methods: Social Science Research in Motion*, by Charlotte Bates. Routledge.

Gaudenzi, Sandra. 2013. 'The living documentary: from representing reality to co-creating reality in digital interactive documentary'. Doctoral thesis. https://doi.org/10.25602/GOLD.00007997

References

Graeber, David. 2015. *The Utopia of Rules*. Melville House.

Hale, Charles. 2006. 'Activist research v. cultural critique: Indigenous land rights and the contradictions of politically engaged anthropology'. *Cultural Anthropology* 96–120.

Hancox, Dan. 2019. *Inner City Pressure: The Story of Grime*. William Collins Books.

Harris, Ella. 2016. 'Precarious times and nonlinear thinking: using i-docs to explore the temporary city'. *i-docs*. http://i-docs.org/precarious-times-and-nonlinear-thinking-using-i-docs-to-explore-contemporary-structures-of-feeling/.

Harris, Ella. 2017. 'Encountering urban space live at the floating cinema'. In *Live Cinema: Cultures, Economies, Aesthetics*, by Sarah Atkinson and Helen Kennedy. Bloomsbury Academic.

Harris, Ella. 2019. 'Compensatory cultures of the post-2008 climate mechanisms for crisis times'. *New Formations* 66–87.

Harris, Ella. 2020a. 'Connecting present moments and present eras with interactive documentary'. *Media Theory*.

Harris, Ella. 2020b. *Rebranding Precarity: Pop-Up Culture as the Seductive New Normal*. Zed Books.

Harris, Ella, and Judith Aston. 2022. 'I-docs, crisis and multi-perspectival thinking'. *i-docs*. http://i-docs.org/i-docs-crisis-and-multi-perspectival-thinking/.

Harris, Ella, and Rebecca Coleman. 2020. 'The social life of time and methods: studying London's temporal architecture'. *Time & Society* 604–31.

Harris, Ella, Mel Nowicki, and Katherine Brickell. 2019. 'On-edge in the impasse: inhabiting the housing crisis as structure of feeling'. *Geoforum* 156–64.

Harvey, David. 1990. 'Between space and time: reflections on the geographical imagination'. *Annals of the Association of American Geographers*.

Hawkins, Harriet. 2015. 'Creative geographic methods: knowing, representing, intervening. On composing place and page'. *Cultural Geographies*.

Hawkins, Harriet. 2020. *Geography, Art, Research: Artistic Research in the GeoHumanities*. Routledge.

Highmore, Ben. 2017. *Cultural Feelings: Mood, Mediation and Cultural Politics*. Routledge.

Hunt, Mia. 2014. 'Urban photography/cultural geography: spaces, objects, events'. *Geography Compass*.

Ioanes, Anna. 2017. 'Feeling and form: new theories of affect and aesthetics'. *the minnesota review* 57–70. https://doi.org/10.1215/00265667-4176073.

Jacobs, Jessica. 2013. 'Listen with your eyes; towards a filmic geography'. *Geography Compass*.

Jameson, Fredric. 1991. *Postmodernism, or The Cultural Logic of Late Capitalism*. Verso.

Jones, Erik, and Daniel Kelemen. 2021. 'Failing forward? Crises and patterns of European integration'. *Journal of European Public Policy*.

Jung, Julia. 2022. CobraCollective. https://cobracollective.org/news/exquisite-corpse-process/.

Kara, Helen. 2015. *Creative Research Methods in the Social Sciences*. Policy Press.

Kara, Helen. 2017. 'Identity and power in co-produced activist research'. *Qualitative Research*.

Laing, Oliva. 2021. *Everybody: A Book about Freedom*. Picador.

Latham, Alan, and Derek McCormack. 2009. 'Thinking with images in non-representational cities: vignettes from Berlin'. *Area* 252–62.

Latour, Bruno. 2011. 'Paris, invisible city'. *City, Culture and Society*.

Laurier, Eric, and Barry Brown. 2011. 'The reservations of the editor: The routine work of showing and knowing the film in the edit suite'. *Social Semiotics* 239–57.

Law, John. 2004. *After Method: Mess in Social Science Research*. Routledge.

Law, John, and John Urry. 2004. 'Enacting the social'. *Economy and Society* 390–410.

Lefebvre, Henri. 2004. *Rhythmanalysis: Space, Time and Everyday Life*. Continuum.

Le Guin, Ursula. 2019. *The Carrier Bag Theory of Fiction*. Ignota.

Lewis, Hannah, Peter Dwyer, and Stuart Hodkinson. 2015. 'Hyper-precarious lives: migrants, work and forced labour in the Global North'. *Progress in Human Geography* 580–600.

Lombard, Melanie. 2023. 'The experience of precarity: low-paid economic migrants' housing in Manchester'. *Housing Studies* 307–26.

Lorimer, Jamie. 2010. 'Moving image methodologies for more-than-human geographies'. *Cultural Geographies*.

Lury, Celia, and Nina Wakeford. 2012. *Inventive Methods: The Happening of the Social*. Routledge.

Lury, Celia, Rachel Fensham, Alexandra Heller-Nicholas, Sybille Lammes, Angela Last, Mike Michael, and Emma Uprichard. 2018. *Routledge Handbook of Interdisciplinary Research Methods*. Routledge.

Marovah, Tendayi, and Faith Mkwananzi. 2020. 'Graffiti as a participatory method fostering epistemic justice and collective capabilities among rural youth: a case study in Zimbabwe'. In *Participatory Research, Capabilities and Epistemic Justice*, by Melanie Walker and Alejandra Boni. Springer.

Massey, Doreen. 2012. 'Power-geometry and a progressive sense of place'. In *Mapping the Futures*, by Doreen Massey. Routledge.

Massey, Doreen. 2005. *For Space*. The Open University.

Massey, Doreen. 2008. 'The future of landscape'. https://www.3ammagazine.com/3am/the-future-of-landscape-doreen-massey/

May, John, and Nigel Thrift. 2001. *TimeSpace: Geographies of Temporality*. Psychology Press.

McFarlane, Colin. 2011. 'The city as assemblage: dwelling and urban space'. *Environment and Planning D: Society and Space*.

McLuhan, Marshall. 2001. *Understanding Media: The Extensions of Man*. MIT Press.

Mehta, Jigar. 2012. '18 Days In Egypt: How We Launched Our Web-Native Documentary'. *Tribeca*. https://tribecafilm.com/news/5136579a1c7d7698e9000017-18-days-in-egypt-how-we-l

Merchant, Stephanie. 2011. 'The body and the senses: visual methods, videography and the submarine sensorium'. *Body & Society*.

Messina, Baris Cayli. 2022. 'Breaking the silence on femicide: how women challenge epistemic injustice and male violence'. *British Journal of Sociology* 859–84.

Mikelli, Danai. 2021. 'Pedagogy of difference 2.0: interactive documentary practices and participatory research with young people'. *Convergence: The International Journal of Research into New Media Technologies*.

Miles, Adrian. 2014. 'Materialism and interactive documentary'. *Studies in Documentary Film* 205–20.

Mkwananzi, Faith, and F. Melis Cin. 2021. *Post-Conflict Participatory Arts: Socially Engaged Development (Rethinking Development)*. Routledge.

Mulholland, Marcela. 2020. 'A moment of intersecting crises: climate justice in the era of coronavirus'. *National Library of Medicine* 257–61.

Murphy, Susan. 2021. 'Climate change and political (in)action: an intergenerational epistemic divide?' *Environmental Management and Conservation*.

Nash, Kate. 2022. *Interactive Documentary: Theory and Debate*. Routledge.

Nelson, Maggie. 2022. *On Freedom*. Penguin.

Nuñez-Janes, Mariela, Aaron Thornburg, Angela Booker, Izabella Penier, Sam Pack, and Adam Leverton, eds. 2017. *Deep Stories: Practising, Teaching, and Learning Anthropology with Digital Storytelling*. De Gruyter.

O'Callaghan, Cian. 2012. 'Lightness and weight'. *Area* 200–7.

O'Flynn, Siobhan. 2015. *Designed Experiences in Interactive Documentaries*. Routledge.

O'Sullivan, Simon. 2001. 'The aesthetics of affect: thinking art beyond representation'. *Angelaki-Journal of the Theoretical Humanities* 125–35. https://doi.org/10.1080/09697250120087987.

Peterle, Giada. 2021. *Comics as a Research Practice: Drawing Narrative Geographies beyond the Frame*. Routledge.

Pickerill, Jenny. 2021. *Methods for Change: Participatory Activist Research*. University of Manchester Press.

Pink, Sarah. 2001. *Doing Visual Ethnography: Images, Media and Representation in Research*. SAGE.

Pink, Sarah. 2007. 'Walking with video'. *Visual Studies* 240–52.

Pink, Sarah. 2015. *Doing Sensory Ethnography*. SAGE.

Pottinger, Laura. 2021. *Methods for Change: Gentle Methodologies*. University of Manchester Press.

Proctor, Robert N., and Londa Schiebinger. 2008. *Agnotology: The Making and Unmaking of Ignorance*. Stanford University Press.

Rainie, Lee, and Barry Wellman. 2012. *Networked: The New Social Operating System*. MIT Press.

Ryan, Kathleen, and David Staton. 2022. *Interactive Documentary: Decolonizing Practice-Based Research*. Routledge.

Sartre, Jean-Paul. 1946. *Existentialism Is a Humanism*. https://warwick.ac.uk/fac/cross_fac/complexity/people/students/dtc/students2011/maitland/philosophy/sartre-eih.pdf

Sharma, Sarah. 2014. *In the Meantime: Temporality and Cultural Politics*. Duke University Press.

Shaw, Ian Graham Ronald, and Barney Warf. 2009. 'Worlds of affect: virtual geographies of video games'. *Environment and Planning A: Economy and Space*.

Simpson, Paul. 2012. 'Apprehending everyday rhythms: rhythmanalysis, time-lapse photography, and the space–times of street performance'. *Cultural Geographies*.

Smith, Shawn Michelle, and Sharon Sliwinski. 2017. *Photography and the Optical Unconscious*. Duke University Press.

Walker, Melanie, and Alejandra Boni. 2020. *Participatory Research, Capabilities and Epistemic Justice*. Palgrave Macmillan.

Weizman, Eyal. 2006. 'The art of war: Deleuze, Guattari, Debord and the Israeli Defence Force.' *Metamute*. https://www.metamute.org/editorial/articles/art-war-deleuze-guattari-debord-and-israeli-defence-force.

Williams, Raymond. 2011. *The Long Revolution*. Parthian.

Ypi, Lea. 2021. *Free: Coming of Age at the End of History*. Penguin.

Index

References to tables appear in **bold** type.

18 Days in Egypt 3, 32
Arab Spring 3, 32, 87, 99, 101–2
co-creative i-doc 87, 99, 101–3
content 101, 102
Mehta, Jigar 101–2

A

activism 8, 98
  activist i-docs and epistemic
    justice 99–104
  activist methods 18, 87
  activist projects 15, 87, 105
  'scholar activism' 103
aesthetics (i-docs) 18, 19, 51–5,
  107–8
  aesthetic design 51, 55, 57, 59, 60,
    68, 117, 118
  affect and atmospheres 19, 51
  affect theory and 54
  affective atmospheres **52**, 55,
    56–60, **113**
  Canva and 116
  Corona Haikus 54
  foregrounding device **52**, 53
  Genially and 118
  *Highrise: The Universe
    Within* 53
  ideation notes for 55
  i-doc planning template **113**
  i-docs as research method 51, 53,
    60, 68
  invited mode of
    spectatorship **52**, 54
  key terms **52**
  localised affects **52**, 56, 60, 68
  The Lockdown Game 46, 53, 60–8,
    93–4, 95
  Migrant Mothers of Syria 53
  minimalist styles 53–4

moods and affects 19, 51, 52–3,
  56, 60, **113**
orientation device **52**, 55, 61, **113**
pervasive affects **52**, 56
Refugee Republic 53
Seven Deadly Digital Sins 54
structures of feeling 51–2, 60, 68
The Temporary City 53, 56–60, 68
  see also The Lockdown Game; The
    Temporary City
affect theory 52, 54, 56–7
agency
  agency frustration 70, 73–4,
    76–8, 80
  Gaza Sderot 42–3
  i-docs and 14, 24, 69
  i-docs engagement: 'notice –
    decide – do' schema 72
  interactivity and 69, 72–3, 76
  Refugee Republic 44
agnotology 100–1
Ahmed, Sara 52
AHRC (Arts and Humanities
  Research Council) 27, 28
  see also StoryArcs
AI (artificial intelligence) 9, 15,
  101, 116
Anderson, Benedict **52**, 56–7, 98
AR and VR projects (augmented
  reality and virtual reality) 4,
  14–15
Arab Spring 13, 33
  18 Days in Egypt 3, 32, 87,
    99, 101–2
Ash, James 11, 17, 73
Aston, Judith 5, 98–9, 104, 109, 111
Athens Report (co-creative i-doc) 87,
  99, 101, 102–3
  content 102

133

crowdsourcing contributions 102
Greek debt crisis 87, 99, 102
map design 102

B

Benjamin, Walter 11
Berger, John 11
Berlant, Lauren 52
Blade Runner (film) 13
Boxing Life (interactive collage) 119

C

Campt, Tina 10–11
Camus, Albert 63
  The Plague 63
Canva (platform) 108, 110, 115–18
Chang, Anita Wen-Shin: *Third Digital Documentary* 15
The Chicago 00 Project 4
Cizek, Katerina, and William Uricchio: *Collective Wisdom* 8, 15, 100
co-creative i-doc making 19, 108
  18 Days in Egypt 87, 99, 101–3
  activist i-docs and epistemic justice 99–104
  Athens Report 87, 99, 101, 102–3
  co-creation and multi-perspectivity 85–7
  collective thinking tool 3, **86**, 87
  countering epistemic injustice 85, 87, 99–100, 103, 105
  different experiences and opinions 8, 19, 62, 63, 85, 86, 95, 96, 105
  finding common ground 8, 19, 85, 97, 98, 102, 105, 108
  i-docs as research method 8, 19, 68, 86, 96–7, 100, 103–4, 105
  imagined community **86**, 97–8
  key terms **86**
  The Lockdown Game 3, 44–5, 62, 71, 77, 83, 86, 87
  The Lockdown Game: audiences and imagined communities 97–9
  The Lockdown Game: shared worlds for difference 63, 87–97
  participatory i-doc making and collective visioning 8, 19
  shared spaces for difference **86**, 87–97
  stories with multiple heroes 104–5

StoryArcs 104–5
  values of 91, 96–7
Coleman, Rebecca, and Jessica Ringrose: *Deleuze and Research Methodologies* 14
comic books 6, 11–12
Corona Haikus 54
Cosgrove, Denis 11
COVID-19 pandemic 3, 17, 54
  freedoms 71
  structure of feeling 57, 71
  see also The Lockdown Game
Crary, Jonathan 10, 11, 16, 34–5
creativity
  creative media as method 8, 9
  creative research methods 7–8, 15
  i-docs as creative method 6–8, 9, 16
Cummings, Dominic 49, 65, 68

D

De Beauvoir, Simone 64
Deep Stories 6
DeLanda, Manuel **38**, 42
Deleuze, Gilles, **22**, 29, 32–3, **38**, 42
DeSilvey, Caitlin 13–14
Deuze, Mark 2
Digital Cultures Research Centre (University of the West of England, Bristol) 5
Digital Me 76–7
digital media 1, 6, 32, 85
Dijn, Annelien de 71
Dovey, Jon 5

E

encountering the world
  creative media and 1
  creative methods and 7, 8
  'encountering the world with i-docs' 7, 20, 84, 107, 110, 119
  technologies and 1–2
Epistemic Fragmentation (interactive collage) 116–18
epistemology
  activist i-docs and epistemic justice 99–104
  co-creative i-docs and countering epistemic injustice 85, 87, s99–100, 103, 105
  epistemic divides 1, 2, 10, 11, 12, 17, 18, 99
  epistemic justice, definition 18, 99
  epistemological fragmentation 100

Index

Existentialism 63–4
The Lockdown Game: Existential realisation 82

F

Fahim, Joseph 13
Favero, Paolo 16, 72
films/cinema 1, 8, 9
  Arab cinema 13
  creative methods and political intent 15
  i-docs: filmic content 21, 27–8, 54
  i-docs: filmic form 32
  non-linear films 110
  Palestinian filmmakers 13
  temporality and 21, 22, 35, 37
freedom 71
  i-docs and digital freedom 72, 76–7
  interactivity: freedom and compliance 7, 19, 69, 71–6
  The Lockdown Game: freedom and compliance 71, 77–84
Freire, Paulo 86
Fricker, Miranda 18, 99, 100, 101

G

Gaudenzi, Sandra 5, 32
  template (the !F Lab Field Guide) 114
Gaza Sderot
  agency 42–3
  complicity compulsion 74
  map view, timeline view, face view, topic view 41–2
  spatial infrastructure 38, 40–3, 44
Genially (platform) 108, 110, 115–16, 118–19
Going North 4
Graeber, David 82
Guardian (newspaper) 54
Guattari, Felix **22**, 29

H

Hale, Charles 103
Hancox, Dan 13
Harris, Ella
  2016 blog 110–11
  2022 blog 111
  Rebranding Precarity 27, 30
  see also *Boxing Life*; *Epistemic Fragmentation*; *The Lockdown Game*; *The Temporary City*

Harvey, David: *The Condition of Postmodernity* 13
Hawkins, Harriet 7, 8
Highrise 3
The Thousandth Tower 72
The Universe Within 3, 53, 76
Hollow 26–7, 32
How to Create a Financial Crisis 74–5

I

I Can Almost See the Lights of Home 4
i-docs (interactive documentaries) 2
  agency and 14, 24, 69
  definition 2, 5, 32
  distinction between i-doc and other web platforms 5
  'encountering the world with i-docs' 7, 20, 84, 107, 110, 119
  filmic content 21, 27–8, 54
  filmic form 32
  game-like platforms 2, 39, 40
  immersive nature of 5
  installation i-docs 4
  non-fiction nature of 2
  non-linear format 17, 29, 32–4, 35, 59, 73, 96, 110
  as offshoot of traditional documentary film 6
  perception and 2, 7, 14
  political intent 15
  scholarship on 5, 16, 32
  site-specific i-docs 4
  as storytelling 91–2, 104
  web-based i-docs 2, 4, 108
i-docs: budget 3, 92, 95, 105, 108, 110
  low-budget projects 107, 109
i-docs: challenges 23, 105, 108
  access to media technologies 105, 109
  activist projects 105
  budget 105, 108, 109
  keeping i-docs alive online 3, 25, 108–9
  technical skills 108
i-docs: components 18
  attention and 18, 19
  particular topics 19
  see also aesthetics; interactivity; spatial infrastructure; temporal architecture
'I-Docs, Crisis and Multi-Perspectival Thinking' (symposium) 111

i-docs: making 2–3, 6–7, 19
  easy-to-use tools 105
  form/meaning relationship 39
  Genially and Canva platforms 108, 110, 115–19
  i-doc editing 29
  i-doc-making limitations 23, 105, 108
  i-doc planning 2, 7
  i-docs as research method 2, 7, 35, 39, 50
  low-budget projects 107, 109
  lower tech alternatives 19, 23, 105, 107, 109–10, 115–19
  power/space relationships and 37–8, 40–50
  temporal architectures and 29, 35
  see also 'thinking with i-docs'
i-docs as research method 1, 2, 3–8, 17–18, 27, 107–8, 119
  aesthetics 51, 53, 60, 68
  attention and perception 7, 14
  co-creative i-docs 8, 19, 68, 86, 96–7, 100, 103–4, 105
  collective thinking 8, **86**, 87, 114
  creating new perceptual equipment 11, 12, 17, 119
  expressing conditions of contemporary world 14, 17, 110–11
  historical context and 9–10, 12
  i-doc making 2, 7, 35, 39, 50
  i-doc planning 2, 7
  i-doc potentials 2, 16
  i-docs as creative method 6–8, 9, 16
  interactivity 69, 73, 77, 84
  intersecting crises and epistemic divides/compounded precarities 1, 2, 10, 11, 12, 17–18, 98–9, 107, 110, 111
  'messy methods' 73
  participant action research 6, 7
  producing changes in the world 16, 17
  spatial infrastructure and power/space relationships 37–8, 40–50
  temporal architectures and 24, 25, 29, 31–2, 35
  visual ethnographic methods and 7
  see also media and research; research; 'thinking with i-docs'
  immersion 2, 5, 30, 58

Instagram 11, 47
interactivity (i-docs) 2, 18, 19, 108
  absence of 42, 69, 75, 84
  agency and 69, 72–3, 76
  agency frustration **70**, 73–4, 76–8, 80
  call to action **70**, 73, **114**
  complicity compulsion 70, 74–5
  Digital Me 76–7
  freedom and compliance 7, 19, 69, 71–6
  Genially and 116, 118
  ideation notes for 75
  i-doc planning template **113–14**
  i-docs and digital freedom 72, 76–7
  i-docs' political potential as media form and 72–3
  i-docs as research method 69, 73, 77, 84
  interactive capacities 7, 19, 51, 69, 71, 74, 75, 77, 84, **113**, **114**
  key terms **70**
  limitations on interactivity 74, 77, **114**
  The Lockdown Game 46, 47, 49, 65
  The Lockdown Game: freedom and compliance 71, 77–84
  Migrant Mothers of Syria 73
  Prison Valley 72–3
  as system of governance 84
  The Thousandth Tower (*Highrise*) 72
  Universe Within (*Highrise*) 76
  UX **70**
  'zugzwang' ('compulsion to move') **70**, 74
the internet 9, 34, 65, 101

J

Jameson, Fredric 10, 12, 119
A Journal of Insomnia 25–6
Journey to the End of Coal 32
Jung, Julia 12

K

Kara, Helen 7
Keiller, Patrick 15

L

Laing, Olivia 71
The Last Generation 26–7
Latour, Bruno: *Paris, Invisible City* 12
Law, John 9, 14, 73
Le Guin, Ursula 99

Index

Life is Beautiful (film) 62
The Lockdown Game 3
  aesthetics 46, 53, 93–4, 95
  aesthetics: being played by the UK government 53, 64–8
  aesthetics: being playful 53, 60–4
  agency frustration 77–8, 80
  audiences and imagined communities 97–9
  compliance compulsion 80
  'confusing cacophony' 61
  content 47, 61, 62–3, 66, 82, 90–1, 93–5
  COVID-19 lockdown 38, 44, 45, 48–9, 61–4, 65, 67–8, 71, 77–80, 81–2, 87, 90
  design process 44–50, 77, 79, 92, 95
  distinction between who was helping and who was being helped 49
  existential experience 63, 80–4
  freedom and compliance 71, 77–84
  funding 44–5
  game-like elements 47–8, 64–8, 81, 94
  indoor/outdoor spaces 48–50, 61, 91
  interactivity 46, 47, 49, 65, 77–84
  interface as a house and local area 92, 94, 95
  links to external sites 61, 97–8
  lockdown rules 43, 49, 64–5, 67, 68, 77–84, 90, 92, 94, 96, 98
  meters 47–8, 64, 65–8, 77, 78, 94
  Miro board 77
  optional endings 79–80, 81
  participants 45, 62, 67, 87–90, 96
  participatory i-doc 3, 44–5, 62, 71, 77, 83, 86, 87–99
  pathway of discovery 47
  power/space relationship 48–50
  producing changes in participants 82–4, 90
  satire 47, 49, 65, 68, 79, 98
  shared worlds for difference 63, 87–97
  soundscapes 46, 48, 61, 91
  spatial infrastructure 38, 44–50
  temporal architecture 46
  UX 92, 93, 94
  Zoom workshops 45–6, 48, 49, 64–5, 66, 77, 79, 92
Lury, Celia, and Nina Wakeford: *Inventive Methods* 8

M

Massey, Doreen 15, 33, 38, 41
McIntyre, Anne Marie 110
McLuhan, Marshall 9
media (creative media) 1–2
  perception and 1, 9–10, 12, 16
  political intent 15
  temporality and 21, 110
  see also digital media; i-docs; social media
media and research (creative media)
  creating new perceptual equipment 10–12, 14, 119
  creative media as method 8, 9
  expressing changes in logics of the world 12–14
  media technologies and history of ways of seeing 9–10, 12
  producing changes in the world 14–17
Methods for Change project 103–4
Migrant Mothers of Syria 53, 73
Miles, Adrian 29, 72

N

Nash, Kate 39
National Film Board of Canada 2–3, 54
  'Challenge for Change' 15
  see also Highrise
Nelson, Maggie 71
non-linearity 8, 14, 21, 33, 116
  i-docs 17, 29, 32–4, 35, 59, 73, 96, 110
  non-linear films 110
  progressive politics and 33
  space–time as non-linear 32–3
Nuñez-Janes, Mariela 86, 91–2

O

Obama, Barack 56
O'Flynn, Siobhan 74
One Shared House 6
Open University: Stories of Change project 14
oral history 4
Oral History and Digital Humanities 15

P

participatory i-doc *see* co-creative i-doc making

perception
  creating new perceptual equipment (media, i-docs) 10–12, 14, 17, 119
  creative media and 1, 9–10, 12, 16
  i-docs and 2, 7, 14
  media technologies and history of ways of seeing 9–10
  'optical unconscious' 11–12
  'ways of seeing' 11
Peterle, Giada 11–12
photography 8, 9, 11
'post-truth' culture 18, 99, 100
Prison Valley 72–3
Prison X (VR project) 14–15
Proctor, Robert N., and Londa Schiebinger 100

Q

Quipu Project 6

R

Refuge Republic
  aesthetics 53
  agency 44
  hand-drawn maps 43, 53
  spatial infrastructure 38, 40, 43–4
research
  activist methods 18, 87
  creative research methods 7–8, 9, 15
  'messy methods' 73
  'ontology politics' of methods 14
  participant action research 6, 7, 15
  research for change 103–4, 105
  story-based methods 86
  see also i-docs as research method; media and research
RooTongue (transmedia project) 4

S

Sartre, Jean-Paul 64, 82
'S'cape' (group of French teachers) 118
Scott, Jack 44, 46, 91, 92
Seven Deadly Digital Sins 54
Sharma, Sarah 22, 24–5
Skelly, Michael 70
  The Lockdown Game 44, 92–5
  The Temporary City 28, 32
Smith, Joe: Stories of Change (interactive digital project) 6
social media 1, 5, 17, 76, 101, 102
Soyinka, Bambo 104

space, definition 41
spatial infrastructure 18, 22, 37–9, 107
  attractors 38, 42
  'database' i-docs 39, 40
  definition 37
  discovery pathways 38, 39, 40, 43, 47, 112
  fluidity/fixity politicised tensions 37, 38, 43–4
  game-like i-docs 39, 40
  Gaza Sderot 38, 40–3, 44
  ideation notes for 39–40
  i-doc making and power/space relationships 37–8, 40–50
  i-doc planning template 112–13
  i-doc typology 39, 113
  key terms 38
  The Lockdown Game 38, 44–50
  map-based i-docs 39, 40, 43, 44
  power geometries 38, 40–50
  Refuge Republic 38, 40, 43–4
  scrolling 39, 112
StoryArcs (AHRC-funded programme, Bath Spa University) 3, 87, 104–5
Story Associates 104–5
Story Skill Set 104–5
structures of feeling 9, 51–2, 56–7, 60, 68
  COVID-19 pandemic 57, 71

T

technology 1–2, 7
  see also AI; media; media and research
temporal architecture (i-docs) 18, 19, 107
  the actual 22, 29
  Canva and 118
  design of i-docs digital interface 22–4
  examples of 25–7
  Genially and 118
  ideation notes for 23
  i-doc planning template 112
  i-docs as research method 24, 25, 29, 31–2, 35
  key terms 22
  The Lockdown Game 46
  non-linearity 32–4, 35, 59
  problematising assumptions about temporality 32–5
  scrolling down 26–7

Index

temporal architecture (term) **22**, 23–5, 29, 31–2, 35
temporal politics 19, 21
temporality 21–5, 29
The Temporary City 27–32, 57
the virtual **22**, 29
see also The Temporary City
temporality
 films 21, 22, 35, 37
 media and 21, 110
 see also non-linearity; temporal architecture; *The Temporary City*
The Temporary City 3
 Adobe Premiere Pro and Adobe Photoshop 27–8, 33–4, 59
 aesthetics 53, 56–60, 68
 affective atmospheres 53, 56, 57–60
 agency frustration 74
 contents of 58
 critique of theoretical assumptions about time 25, 33–5
 digital interface 28
 filmic content and editing clips 27–9
 housing crisis 34, 59–60
 immersion 30, 58
 making of: rationale 27–9
 'outside pop-up city' pages 33–5, 58–60
 pop-up culture 30–2, 57, 58
 pop-up culture: non-linear temporal imaginaries 33–4
 pop-up culture, temporality of 25, 27, 30–2
 pop-up places 27, 31, 34, 53, 57
 precarity and pop-up 34, 53, 57, 60

'Pulp Kitchen' clip (*Pulp Fiction* film and) 58, 59
secrecy and surprise 31, 58, 59, 60
'The Ship's Kitchen' clip 59–60
temporal architecture design 27–32, 57
video ethnography and interviews 27
see also temporal architecture
Terminal 3 4
'thinking with i-docs' 19, 107, 109, 119
i-doc planning template 19, 109, 111–15
 prompts **112–14**
 research topic 114, 115
 see also i-docs: making
TikTok 11
Typeform (app) 117

U

Urry, John 14
UX (user experience) 30, **70**, 92, 93, 94

V

video games 11, 13, 17, 73, 94
Visme 116

W

The Waiting Room 4
Weizman, Eyal 33
Williams, Raymond 9, 12, 56
Witness 360: 7/7 4

Y

Ypi, Lea 71

www.ingramcontent.com/pod-product-compliance
Lightning Source LLC
Chambersburg PA
CBHW071715020426
42333CB00017B/2275